For Pat
Best wishes
[illegible signature]
2/17/05

Capital Tennis

Capital Tennis

A Memoir

Allie Ritzenberg

Founder and director of the
St. Albans Tennis Club

THE FRANCIS PRESS

WASHINGTON, D.C.

Printed in the United States of America

FIRST EDITION

Library of Congress Cataloging-in-Publication Data

Ritzenberg, Allie, 1918–
Capital tennis : a memoir / Allie Ritzenberg.-- 1st ed.
p. cm.
Includes index.
ISBN 0-9665051-9-0 (hardcover)
1. Ritzenberg, Allie, 1918- 2. Tennis players--Washington (D.C.)
I. Title.
GV994.R58A3 2004
796.342'092--dc22

2004022054

The International Tennis Hall of Fame, in Newport, Rhode Island, which acquired the Albert and Madeleine Ritzenberg Collection of tennis antiquities in June 2004, has permitted the reproduction of the photographs of various pieces of the collection that appear in this book.

Frontispiece photo:
First Stained Glass Depicting Tennis
Once installed at an Adirondack spa,
with original wood frame and with original leading
ARTIST UNKNOWN
circa 1875 63" x 36"

Book and jacket design by Kathleen Sims

Published by The Francis Press
Washington, DC
www.francispress.com

In Recognition

Of my friend Joe Howell who lent his editorial expertise
at a critical phase in the development of this book
and helped shape the entire manuscript.

Dedication

To my life's companion Peg and
our four wonderful children,
Ken, Frank, Fred, and Kate.

In Memoriam

Nate Ritzenberg (1916–2003)

A free spirit who created his own style of living and
remained true to his ideals until the very end.

Contents

Prologue

In 1961, I received a phone call from Tish Baldridge, the social secretary at the Kennedy White House. Because Tish was a regular tennis player at the courts where I was a pro at the time, I assumed she was calling about her court reservation. But, Tish explained, her purpose was to invite me to the White House to give a tennis lesson to the First Lady the very next day. Before I had a chance to respond, I realized that I was already committed to teach youngsters enrolled in an inner-city tennis program. A small voice in my head said, "Drop everything, you fool, and go." But my conscience won out. I told Tish about my dilemma and offered to respond to her summons on another day. "There goes the chance of a lifetime," I thought, doubting that I would ever get another call.

But as luck would have it, Tish consented to my request and the lesson was rescheduled. On the appointed day, I put on a new sweater, my good tennis shoes, and shirt and trousers and appeared at the White House gate looking my very best. The guards had been told to expect me, and they pointed me in the direction of the tennis court. Nervously I awaited the arrival of the most famous and most glamorous pupil I would ever teach. No one was in sight.

While I pondered the correct protocol (should I say, "I'm honored to meet you, Mrs. Kennedy," not my style, or simply, "How do you do, Mrs. Kennedy"), I spotted two women with a small white terrier walking from the mansion toward the tennis courts. They were too distant to be recognizable. Suddenly the dog bolted away and made a beeline toward some ducks that were waddling around on the White House lawn. One of the women shrieked and launched in hot pursuit of the canine, who I imagined was entertaining visions of a raw duckling dinner. I immediately joined in the chase and was able to get my hands on the dog's hindquarters and then to pry open his jaws. After a few growls and barks to demonstrate his displeasure at my failure to mind my own business, he resigned himself to his misfortune and calmed down.

In completing my mission, I had fallen on my hands and knees. From this undignified position, I looked into the eyes of Jacqueline Kennedy—big, dark eyes, so unmistakable from their endless replications on magazine covers, on television, and in newspaper photographs. My distress at being on all fours for my introduction to the First Lady was somewhat alleviated by the fact that she, too, was on her hands and knees. We both scrambled to our feet as she tried to brush the grass stains off her white slacks. She thanked me for my heroics and we both laughed at the circumstances of our first meeting.

The First Lady then introduced me to her amused companion, Toni Bradlee, the wife of Ben Bradlee, then head of the Washington bureau of *Newsweek,* who later gained fame as the executive editor of *The Washington Post* and directed its coverage of the Watergate scandals.

This event was the first of numerous visits to the White House that introduced me to many in the Kennedy extended family and the Kennedy administration who would become members of the St. Albans Tennis Club that I founded the following year.

Located on the beautiful hilltop grounds of the National Cathedral in northwest Washington, about three miles from the White House and five miles from the Capitol, St. Albans School is one of the city's elite private schools. Its students are boys in the fourth through twelfth grades. In the spring of 1962 I worked out an arrangement with Canon Charles Martin, then headmaster of the school, to be both coach of the school's tennis program and director of a new tennis club. The club would have access to the ten St. Albans courts before and after school hours and on weekends and holidays. The busy New Frontiersmen and women could take lessons or play at St. Albans in the mornings and still get to work by the time official Washington began to function.

Because so many people started playing in the 7:00 A.M. time slot, *The Washington Post* declared that early morning tennis at St. Albans was the "in thing" in the nation's capital, an observation that *Sports Illustrated* echoed when reporting a similar tennis boom all across the country. The magazine traced the origin of the tennis boom to St. Albans and the high-profile pupils and members playing there. The young, dynamic group from the Kennedy White House certainly blazed a tennis trail that millions followed, and tennis was an important part of that short period of American history that we call Camelot.

Over the years, the St. Albans Tennis Club has become a place where many highly placed government officials, both Democrats and Republicans, as well as a good number of Washington "power lawyers," journalists, and business leaders, have chosen to play tennis, and I have been fortunate to get to know most of them. Of course, a majority of club members have not been high-profile politicians and celebrities but other people from all walks of life and with varying tennis abilities. Needless to say many of the "low-profile" members are my friends as well.

I have also been fortunate to play tennis competitively. I learned to play tennis in the parks and playgrounds of Washington, not in the country clubs, and had only one tennis lesson my entire life. My brother Nate and I seemed to pick up tennis naturally and learned from watching some of the good players in the city, many of whom we soon were able to beat on a regular basis. I played tennis at the University of Maryland, where I lost only a couple of times during my entire college career. Returning to Washington after World War II, I decided to become a professional tennis teacher. The big tournaments were not open to both amateurs and professionals until the 1968 United States Open, but by that time I was fifty years old. That was too old to compete in the major tournaments, but just the right age for seniors competition, which was becoming popular. So I decided to compete again seriously, at the seniors level. And over the last thirty-plus years I have participated in almost every major national and international seniors tournament, winning my fair share of them in both singles and doubles. Currently I am ranked number one in the world among players eighty-five and older.

About the same time that I started competing as a senior I became very interested in collecting what I call "tennis-inspired art," and I have spent a great deal of time on tour or on vacation or on weekends looking for works of art, artifacts, or other historical items that relate to tennis. My collection today is one of the largest and, I believe, best collections of such art in the world, and I have found great satisfaction in this pursuit. In June 2004, the entire collection was acquired by the International Tennis Hall of Fame in Newport, Rhode Island.

While the St. Albans Tennis Club has remained remarkably the same over the past forty years, extraordinary changes in the political and cultural life of my city and the nation have occurred during this time, as well as changes in the game that I love. Some of these changes have been for the better. Some have been for the worse. I am just happy that through it all I have been able to play the game.

Helen Wills Moody
Bronze figurine
ENID FOSTER
1924 13" x 6" x 7"

CHAPTER 1

The Early Years

As guns were being silenced after years of heavy fighting, at approximately eleven o'clock on the eleventh day of the eleventh month in 1918, Armistice Day, my mother gave birth to me eleven years to the day after the birth of her oldest child. In the intervening years, she had two other sons and one daughter. By the time I arrived, my father, Sam Ritzenberg, had built a small business as a hardware store owner. His store was on Pennsylvania Avenue about five blocks west of the White House. Because of this proximity, he was the one who was called when President and Mrs. Harding returned home from a trip to discover that they had lost the key to their trunk, which contained some of the First Lady's favorite gowns. My father immediately went to the White House and examined the lock; but not wanting to make the solution seem too simple, he played around a bit with the lock and key. Then, like a magician, presto, he opened the trunk, to the joy of the president's wife.

My father was born and raised in a medium-sized town on the Russian-Polish border. He was educated in the ghetto Hebrew school, where he was noted for his beautiful penmanship. After being drafted into the Russian army and surviving a number of pogroms, he emigrated to America, arriving in the States in 1904 with virtually no money.

My mother came from a totally different background. She was a Kohan who traced her roots back to ancient Hebrew high priests. For centuries the Kohanim had been Hebrew teachers for whom education was a guiding principle of life. Honesty was also a very important value: I remember my grandmother walking a long distance to return a very small amount of money a merchant had mistakenly overpaid her in change.

"Mama," as we called my mother, toiled for the family. She cooked, washed, ironed, shopped, sewed, and gave her life for her children and her husband. She was very conscious about diet and served only healthy foods. We didn't eat much meat and everything was as fresh as she could find. She would take the streetcar a long way to the market and bring back several shopping bags filled with food. The chickens, I remember, were alive. One of my jobs was to take them down the alley to be slaughtered in the ritualized kosher style by Rabbi Yoelson, who had been given a large house by his famous son, entertainer and movie star, Al Jolson.

My mother's interest in healthy food had a big influence on me and my siblings; Several of us have been vegetarians practically all our adult lives.

My father was a small businessman and shrewd competitor. A similar hardware store once opened in the adjoining building and the owner placed a sign over his door reading "Entrance." When my father began losing customers to the new store, he countered by putting up a sign over his door that read "Main Entrance."

My family maintained strong spiritual values, but we lost the formal side of Judaism. In fact, I was over twenty-one when I first went into a house of worship, when a lady friend insisted that I accompany her to the Friend's Meeting House on Florida Avenue in northwest Washington. I found the service to be somewhat strange, with not much going on and never attended another Quaker service—or many other religious services for that matter, except for weddings and funerals.

My athletic career started early. When I was five or six, my brothers took me to a July 4th festival with a track meet and I won the race for children. I participated in the sectional and city track meets at what was then a playground across from Union Station. Competing in the 50 to 70-pound division, I set a city record in the running broad jump with a distance of 13 feet 6 inches. I played softball, but with hardball rules and without gloves. We also played some football in the zoo park but that wasn't really my sport. I was too small and didn't get a growth spurt until I was sixteen.

My sport, it turned out, would be tennis. Actually I had only one tennis lesson, when I was sixteen, and that didn't amount to much. I started off by watching others hit and then by practicing along with my brother Nate, who was about two years older than I, taking our cues from the successful players. Tennis was often impeded because we kept breaking the strings of the cheap rackets that the playground provided. The tennis director at the playground was Walter Haight, who later wrote the horse racing column for *The Washington Post.* He devised a method of replacing the broken strings, which in the days before nylon were made of silk, with a solid piece of wood. When I started playing at the playground, I used a sawed-off racket.

When I was eleven, I was starting to get pretty good and won the Henry D. Cook School Playground Tennis Championship in the Adams Morgan neighborhood by beating Finn Mattingly in the finals. I wasn't much higher than the net, and Finn was about sixteen years old and close to six feet tall. The prize was a pint of very creamy ice cream from a fancy bakery nearby. I had a tough time eating it all. Finn's reward was a Popsicle, which as it turned out was not much consolation because his father owned a neighborhood pharmacy where he could get all the Popsicles he wanted.

Not all my tennis was played at the school yard. My oldest brother Hy delivered mail for the post office while attending a local law school at night. At school he had a friend who roomed with a student at Georgetown University Dental School who was one of Washington's better tennis players. My next oldest brother, Nate, and I tagged along with Hy when he went to the tennis courts in his miniature Austin automobile, and we became so enamored with the game that we went from court to court trying to get some playing time. For a city of its size in those prewar years, Washington actually had a good number of public tennis courts available either for free or for a fee of ten cents per hour.

Bob Considine was the city champion and became one of my idols. He grew up in the poor end of Washington near Union Station but was given a scholarship by George Washington University, where he spent most of his time playing tennis. He came up with an idea to write a tennis column, which he presented to Shirley Povich at the *Post* and which eventually led to the Sunday column, "On the Line with Considine," which he used in part to talk about the local interest in tennis. My brother Nate and I were mentioned in many of those articles, which inspired us to keep playing tennis.

Other players also had a strong influence on me. One was Clarence Charest, a prominent lawyer with the Treasury Department, who had been the top player in town before Considine and had won a number of championships playing with just one arm, as he had lost an arm in World War I. He had to switch from being a right-handed player to a left-handed player. By holding the ball on his racket and tossing it in the air, he was able to serve. He later went on to become a three-time winner of the United States Seniors Championship for the forty-five and over group. He was not only a great tennis player but a true gentleman on and off the court. Those were great days, playing tennis in the park with Nate and beating many people much older and more experienced than ourselves.

I also spent a lot of time working for my father in his junk business. He was a true optimist, a trait that he instilled in me. Unfortunately, in his case, optimism carried over to a devotion to gambling and taking risks. After being introduced to the racetrack by a friend and having a very lucky inaugural day, he got hooked. He spent a lot of time in the mid-1920s going off to south Florida where there was lots of horse racing—and also potentially a bright economic future—though it was more the horse racing than the future that drew my father to Florida. He also played poker and pinochle regularly.

THE GREAT DEPRESSION

In the late 1920s we lived in a middle-class house in the Adams Morgan section of Washington not far from the National Zoo. But soon after the Great Depression hit, my father found himself on hard times. I can still vividly recall the sign on our front yard and the red flag in front of our house as it went up for auction and we were forced to move.

We moved to New York in the early 1930s when my father managed to find work with his brother, who was constructing an apartment house in the Forest Hills section of New York City. We moved to a house near the border of Brooklyn and Queens and I was enrolled in the final semester of grade school at PS224. My most vivid memory there was the assembly when students marched with long strides down both aisles of the deeply sloped floor loudly singing "Onward Christian Soldiers." As a Jew I felt very uncomfortable when I heard the words of the Lord's Prayer that was said every morning at the start of school.

Upon graduation, I was asked to attend the Stuyvesant High School for Gifted Students, but my parents didn't want me to take the train every day to Manhattan so I ended up at the John Adams Public High School in Queens, near the Aqueduct Race Track and close to where Kennedy Airport is today.

In New York, I continued playing tennis along with my brother Nate and managed to land a spot on the tennis team where I was probably the smallest person ever to be awarded a letter. Before long Nate and I were dominating our age group playing tennis in Forest Park and Highland Park, which were both located near Forest Hills, the traditional site of the United States National Tennis Championships. The courts there were public and had a clay surface; and even after the balls got worn down, they continued to be used. The wool nap disappeared, making the balls lighter and less wind resistant so that the balls sailed farther and were not as easily controlled. In order to control the depth of a shot with these worn-out balls, the players developed an extremely high, heavy top spin, which made the shots dip quickly. This strategy, which was unorthodox at the time, marked the beginning of a tennis style that eventually came to dominate the sport many years later and is now the style used frequently by good young players. How many of them realize that they are copying a style developed on the public courts of New York City during the Great Depression?

One of the great things about being close to Forest Hills was being able to watch top-notch tennis tournaments. I got to be a ball boy at the United States Nationals and for hours watched the great players of the period and imitated the beautiful forehands of people such as J. Gilbert Hall and Frank Shields, the grandfather of Brooke Shields. I developed my own style by imitating the style of the great players.

BACK TO WASHINGTON

Although my second-oldest brother, Abe, and sister, Sylvia—both of whom were in their twenties—were able to find jobs in New York and would have been happy to stay there, the rest of the family was eager to return to Washington. So in 1934 we returned to where we had lived in the Adams Morgan neighborhood. I entered Central High School in Washington late in my sophomore year. Central—now called Cardoza High School—was a grand old building that stood on the top of a hill on 13th Street overlooking the entire city. It had its own indoor swimming pool, indoor track, large outdoor stadium, and an auditorium with a huge stage. It was a fine institution that graduated many people who went on to excel in their fields.

Most important to me, however, Central had a very good tennis team, which won the city championship. Both Nate and I played on that team and we were the two best junior players, age eighteen and under, in the area. Nate won the D.C. and the Mid-Atlantic championships in 1935, and I won those same two championships in 1936.

I thought that our reputation as good tennis players might give us an advantage getting into a private school. So I approached a school called Devitt Prep—which was located on Upton Steet near Connecticut Avenue in northwest Washington and is now the Edmund Burke School—to see if they would give Nate and me scholarships for the last year of high school. The school was struggling at the time because of low enrollment during the Depression, and the school administration welcomed both of us, hoping that some tennis publicity might boost enrollment. In those days, local sports got a huge play in the newspapers, and tennis tournaments often rated headlines on the sports pages.

When we were at Devitt, Nate and I arranged our tennis schedules so that our team played three singles and two doubles matches against the opposition. Since the Ritzenbergs could beat most local high school players, we were pretty much assured of winning two singles and one doubles match. So we would pick up anyone at the school who wanted to play and fill out the team, not really caring how well they played because we knew we were going to win our matches. Once, for a match against Mercersberg Academy, we had a hard time finding a fifth player. I asked a friend, Allen Ogus, to play for us, knowing he had a friend at the school whom he wanted to visit. The only problem was that Allen did not attend Devitt Preparatory School. When the results were printed in *The Washington Post,* Dr. Ogus was not too happy to find out about his son's participation in the event.

Even though I had enough credits to graduate from Devitt in the middle of the year, the headmaster wanted me to stick around. However, I was becoming restless, and playing tennis would have required me to stay a full year; so I decided to transfer back to Central, where I finished up in February 1937.

During this period my father had taken up a new business, scrap metal and salvage, which never made a fortune but was sufficient to keep the family living fairly comfortably. During the winter months, he would take off to Florida following the horses, and I worked in his shop while he was gone. It was a good education for me because the salvage business required great attention to detail. It was cutthroat, with sellers and buyers using every conceivable dirty trick to get the best of the opposition. Scales were at times manipulated; and the dealer, if he didn't keep alert, could get stuck very easily.

This work gave me a healthy respect for the often poorly educated entrepreneur with guts who could compute figures in his head with machinelike quickness. I saw both the seamy side and the honorable side of the business: the crooks, who had no scruples, and others who were one hundred percent honest. The experience instilled in me many of the values that I still hold today. In that business your word was your bond and you got ahead through hard work and determination.

But when I was eighteen, life suddenly took a major turn for the worse when my mother suffered a severe heart attack. She was hospitalized, and in the usual style of the time, she was restricted from physical activity. But when she was struck again, we decided she should go to a Seventh Day Adventist hospital, which offered much more aggressive treatment. Rather than immobilizing their patients, the doctors gave them hydrotherapy treatment and encouraged them to walk and exercise. The diet was vegetarian and the staff took a genuine interest in the sick. My mother's progress improved, and when her doctor insisted that she live in a home without stairs, we were able to find a one-story bungalow in Chevy Chase, Maryland, just across the D.C. line. Unfortunately, that was not enough. Shortly after we moved in, my mother had an even more serious heart attack that proved fatal. She was just fifty-three. My father, however, would live to be eighty-four and have two more wives.

COLLEGE YEARS

During the period following my mother's death, still in the midst of the Depression, virtually no one could afford to go away to college. Most students went to local schools. I wanted to go to a tennis power, such as the University of North Carolina, but they were not able to offer me a definite scholarship. So I decided to go to the University of Maryland. Several years later, however, I did get some personal satisfaction out of beating the number one player from the University of North Carolina.

The start of my college years marked my separation from Nate, who had graduated from high school ahead of me but decided not to attend college. He moved out of the area to live in the South, where he started to pursue a tennis career of his own, living in Mississippi before finally settling in Florida. He distanced himself not only from me but from the whole family; and even though we both pursued tennis careers, our paths rarely crossed again from the time I finished high school.

The tennis coach at Maryland was Leslie Bopst, who was a chemist and head of the state fertilizer testing lab at College Park. He actually knew very little about the sport. By putting down $50, I was able to register at Maryland with deferred tuition payments, and Coach Bopst also arranged to get me a job that paid $0.35 an hour working at labs cleaning test tubes and installing water lines.

After being accepted to Maryland, I moved near the campus with the help of a housing allowance from the coach. In the summer, I worked on the D.C. playgrounds along with a group of other local athletes, including Red Auerbach, later of Boston Celtics fame. I also got a subsidized job from the federal Works Projects Administration, the WPA, for $37 a week, which involved driving around government officials. I was even able to maintain the job when I returned to Maryland in the fall by getting a driver for $12 a week to do the driving for me. So I was doing fairly well financially because my housing was paid for (a motel room near the university) and I was earning money from the WPA. It all worked pretty well until my driver disregarded my instructions, used the car for personal use, and banged it up.

In 1938 I was invited to accompany my friend Allen Ogus to Woodmont Country Club. Peggy Snowden, just home from school after her sophomore year at the Woman's College of the University of North Carolina at Greensboro, was also a guest. She was playing tennis rather badly and wearing shorts that were causing a problem by slipping. I lent her my belt. The buckle indicated that it was a prize for winning the Southern Conference Intercollegiate Tennis Championship. She may have been impressed, I don't know. But at least she was not too put off, because we started dating.

During my four years on the Maryland tennis team (1938–1941), I lost only four matches, and two of those were while playing injured. I played the number one position; and in the Southern Conference Tournament, I was the top-seeded player in my senior year. In my junior year two of us represented Maryland at the Middle Atlantic Intercollegiate Invitational Championships at the Greenbrier Hotel in White Sulphur Spring, West Virginia, which was then, as it is now, one of the most luxurious resorts in the country. That first year I won the doubles, and the next year I lost in the singles finals. I truly enjoyed the exposure to a lifestyle I had never before experienced, where most of the patrons "dressed" for dinner and seemed to enjoy the good life. The prizes were merchandise from the hotel store, and I picked out a cashmere scarf that seemed eight feet long and two feet wide. I decided I could easily get accustomed to that kind of life. I never dreamed then that my career some years later would put me in daily contact with the same kinds of people who enjoyed the good life at the Greenbrier.

The university was not doing much for tennis players in those days. Most of the extras were coming from Les Bopst's pocket. All of his small salary for coaching seemed to be going to us. He had a relatively good job, which afforded him and his family a nice house, a car, and, unfortunately, all the gin he could drink. When we went on trips, he would stop for gasoline and then go into the men's room with his small travel bag. He drank excessively, but we never saw him drunk.

In my final year, I played at the Naval Academy in the qualifying tournament for a place in the United States National Intercollegiate Championship. The competition was extremely strong, with Joe Hunt, who would become the national champion in 1943, as one of the four to qualify. But as a semifinalist, I still qualified for the Nationals. I called our director of athletics and requested $50 expense money to play at the Merion Cricket Club in Philadelphia. He asked if I was sure I would win the Nationals, to which I replied that I did not think so but would do my best. He did not give me the money.

In the quarterfinals of the qualifying tournament, however, I had defeated Zan Carver of the University of North Carolina who had been a wonderful athlete at St. Albans School in Washington, where I ultimately would end up coaching. Since Zan lived in the immediate vicinity of Merion, I suggested he be my alternate.

He played and reached the quarterfinals, an accomplishment which I like to think meant that I was among the top eight college players in the United States at that time.

In those days the University of Maryland was riddled with racism and anti-Semitism. Fraternities and sororities were separated and it was unheard of for an organization to accept any student from another religion. As a result, the Jewish kids had their own fraternal organizations and segregated themselves. Even the Jewish fraternities were biased, with German or Reform Jews distancing themselves from the Orthodox or Conservative Jews of Eastern Europe.

One day an older athlete asked if he could drive me home to Washington. That seemed to be a charitable gesture, especially coming from Eddie Johnson, the son of Walter Johnson, the famous baseball player. I was not only a tennis player but also played intramural football and boxed. I thought Eddie and I might have a lot in common. Although we were friendly for years, it later dawned on me that the real purpose of this visit was to find out about my personal life—such as where I lived and what my religion was—in order to determine if I was suitable for their fraternity. They never asked me to join—not that I would have wanted to anyway.

Tennis was my main activity at Maryland though I did study for courses that I liked and tended to do pretty well in those subjects. I was most interested by the social sciences like cultural anthropology and sociology; and for that reason I decided to major in sociology with a minor in speech. The speech department was especially progressive at the time, with excellent courses in radio, taught by an inspirational teacher, Ray Ehrensburger, who, after the war, set up branches of the University of Maryland throughout the world. Ray brought in great guest lecturers, many of whom had national reputations and were the stars of the CBS affiliate in Washington.

Those were great years at the University of Maryland, where I really came into my own as a tennis player. The country was coming out of the Depression, and there seemed to be lots of opportunities, but all that would change on December 7, 1941.

THE WAR BREAKS OUT

After finishing college in 1941, I spent the summer teaching tennis at the Woodmont Country Club, a Jewish country club, located at the time in Bethesda, Maryland on the site of what is now the National Institutes of Health. When the tennis season was over, I managed to find a job with a radio station, a local CBS affiliate. One of the perks at the radio station was free tickets to sports and theatrical events. These were called "Annie Oakleys" because the holes punched in them resembled those created by the famous woman sharp shooter.

I was picking up some Annie Oakleys on December 7 when the switchboard operator gave me the news that Pearl Harbor had been bombed. Eric Severeid, the famous CBS correspondent covering the White House, desperately needed a typewriter. So I located one, placed it in a large black bag, hailed a cab, and raced to the White House a few blocks away. Walking hurriedly to the side entrance, I was never challenged or stopped. Times have certainly changed with regard to security!

The next day at the studio we huddled together and listened to President Roosevelt as he made his famous "day of infamy" address to congress. The war had begun.

Because the Selective Service Board had classified me as a 4F due to a calcified tubercle larger than the minimum size (often a sign of having had tuberculosis—which I had not had), I expected to stay in Washington. A tennis friend, who at the time was the employment chief for a government news agency, told me he was desperate for help and that I would be able to work into a position writing news copy for the government. This sounded like a good opportunity so I decided to take the job though it did not take me long to realize that my goal would probably not be realized because many important journalists were already working for the agency, which later would become the Central Intelligence Agency. The job paid $32 a week.

Although we did not use such terms as "propaganda," this is what the office produced. Some of Franklin D. Roosevelt's speeches were written there, and on several occasions I had to deliver speeches to the White House for broadcast that evening. As soon as one or two pages were ready I would start delivering, driving in my own car from the old offices located across from what today is the Department of State. It sometimes took four or five trips before the task was completed; and at each stop, I would glance at the papers, which were not safeguarded in any way, and read what the president was going to say.

The job did not last long because I soon received notice from my draft board that it had made a mistake about the calcified spots and I was now classified as 1A. I immediately was drafted into the army. I was still dating Peg at the time, and while the thought of being away from her for an extended period of time was not pleasant, in those days we had no choice.

After a short stay at Camp Lee in Virginia, I was shipped off to the Army Air Corps basic training program at Keesler Field in Biloxi, Mississippi, where I got my first look at Spanish moss and experienced living in the Deep South. Four of us from the Washington area quickly struck up a friendship. One had been a worker at the Smithsonian and was quite bright. Another was a minor department store executive. The third was an artist, whose latest work was a portrait of General George Marshall that had just been dedicated at the Virginia Military Institute.

The artist, Les Emery, and I were walking through town one day when he stopped in front of an old brick building and mentioned how much he would like to paint a picture of it. I asked why he would want to paint a picture of a horizontal bunch of bricks. He replied that each brick is different. I often quote this story when people want to know why teaching tennis is not boring. It's not boring because two people, like bricks, are never alike, and a good tennis teacher must always modify teaching technique for each player.

After basic training, we were given a choice of schools for specialized education. My friends and I agreed that location was important, so when someone said that Denver was a great place to live, the four of us quickly decided to go as a group to the Air Corps Armament School in Denver. Off we went. However, I did not last long in armaments due to my poor mechanical skills. Before long I was reassigned to another department, the athletic department. So the first several months of my army career were spent playing tennis. I played in the local tennis championships and reached the finals of all three events, losing in the singles to the former national intercollegiate doubles champion, Doug Imhoff of the University of California at Berkeley. I concluded that this might not be such a bad way to spend my time in the army.

Peg was able to come out to the graduate school in Denver, and we enjoyed the surrounding mountains at every opportunity. Because Peg had an uncle who was one of the top officers in the air force, there was pressure for me to "make something of myself" and not be satisfied with the lowly status of an enlisted man. So I applied for Officer Candidate School in Miami Beach, Florida, and was accepted for the ninety-day course. After being in Denver for several weeks I headed for Florida. Our social group of four friends had to split up, and I never saw any of them again. One became an intelligence officer and was later killed in action.

OCS involved a lot of physical, mental, and emotional strain. However, I was young and flexible enough so that I was able to do pretty well and ranked near the top of my class. After the first six weeks, when pressure eased off, the program became easier. At that time Peg and I decided to get married. She came down from Washington, where she had been teaching; and on November 16, 1942, we were married at the Roney Plaza Hotel by a chaplain whose last name was Angel. I hoped that the name would be a positive omen; and it must have been, because we have now been married for more than sixty years. The whole wedding and dinner were accomplished on a three-hour pass. Our only witness was a friend of Peg's from Washington. Newly married soldiers were allowed to use three-hour passes to visit their wives periodically, but the rules forbade any travel other than to the residence of the wife or to a restaurant. It was not the most ideal way to start a marriage, but at least Peg was able to stay near the base.

Six weeks later I received my commission as a second lieutenant and was assigned to the 380th Bomber Group training in El Paso, Texas. Our stay in El Paso was short, however, and we soon were reassigned overseas.

We headed to San Francisco, but Peg was suffering from the measles and was not able to accompany me. We did not know if we would ever see each other again.

A SOLDIER IN AUSTRALIA

The ship we boarded was fast enough to outrun submarines, so in December 1942 my squadron proceeded to Sydney, Australia, without escort. After disembarking, we were put up in tents on a racetrack for about a week. My job was in ground support for the squadron. The several weeks we spent in Sydney were not bad: We had meals with local families, went sightseeing, and even enjoyed opportunities to play tennis. Someone had heard that I was a tennis player and asked if I would like to play against his friend, Jack Crawford, the Australian who had won the Wimbledon championship in 1933. I enthusiastically accepted, borrowed some equipment, and went out to White City, the famous Australian tennis club. Having played only once in the previous six months and not having had much experience on grass, I was not very confident. The preceding several days had been rainy and the grass was quite damp. Since I was rusty, most of my shots were short and because the grass was wet the balls did not bounce very high. Surprisingly, however, I won the first three games, but then lost in straight sets before we stopped for the usual tea.

After two weeks at the camp, we boarded a small "liberty ship," which was escorted as far as the start of the Great Barrier Reef. We were told that a Japanese submarine was lurking nearby but had been repelled. Our ship then proceeded north. After leaving the safety of the reef, it anchored near the northeast tip of Australia. We could not understand why we had to toss around in the waves for several days in one spot. Later we learned that the enemy had knowledge of when and where we were scheduled to land and had bombed the area with antipersonnel "daisy cutters," bombs that sprayed shrapnel in every direction. So being tossed about by the waves was not a bad price to pay for averting disaster. Several days later we weighed anchor and arrived in Darwin on the north coast in the middle of the night, and were immediately placed in trucks, which drove us overland to our destinations. Even though we were in the tropics, the ride in the back of the trucks was chilling.

My squadron was posted at Mambuloo Station, an old ranch near the village of Katherine about one hundred miles southeast of Darwin. The village looked like a miniature wild west movie set, with only three small houses. However, there was a tennis court; and I immediately set off to find out if there was some way that we could put it into use. I followed a sign pointing to the "amenities office" and found the person in charge to be an Australian wearing civilian clothing, which indicated to me that he probably worked for the YMCA or a similar civilian group. When I asked him about tennis, he pointed down the street and told me to see a "bloke by the name of Dyly." I approached this tall red headed officer, who replied in an American accent that his name was "Daley." Soon the tennis court would be put to use.

At OCS it was a common joke about becoming a mess officer, and as luck would have it, that turned out to be one of my first assignments. The job took on a special challenge when I realized how poorly the food operation had been managed and that the financial situation was desperate. After several months I was able to get things back in order, an accomplishment that earned me an immediate promotion. When I got promoted I also got a job change that took me out of the mess hall and into a more interesting job of ground support for the flyers.

Even though the war seemed to be winding down, pilots and crew continued to go on missions, some never to return, others shot up badly, and still others incinerated on the runway as their heavily laden bombers crashed on takeoff. We did not resemble a military force at all. We never paraded and never wore any insignias; but we produced effective wartime work. The group earned several presidential citations, and for a time until B-29s came into use, our B-24 Liberators flew the longest missions of the war when we bombed the oil fields of Balikpapan and other targets in the Dutch East Indies.

We tried to make life as comfortable as possible and for the most part were successful. We stripped one bomber and used it to procure food to supplement our GI rations with milk, fresh vegetables, and even wine. We purchased food on the open market in Adelaide and ferried it on the stripped-down bomber back to our base. One day a pilot wanted to impress his girlfriend, so shortly after takeoff from the grass strip at Adelaide he flew over her house and then pulled up suddenly. Unfortunately, the weight of the food shifted and broke open the bomb-bay doors with milk, fruit, and wine falling out and crashing onto the ground. The next day the Adelaide newspaper carried the story with headlines that read "Manna from Heaven."

Someone suggested that we build a tennis court next to the shack that we had converted into a homemade officers' club. An Australian bulldozer operator, who had been working on the airstrip, agreed to take on the task for several cartons of cigarettes. We also were able to work out a deal with a truck driver who was oiling the dusty roads to spread asphalt on the ground. The asphalt was mixed with sand taken from a nearby crocodile-infested creek. We chopped down trees to use for wooden posts and found chicken wire for fencing. When we completed the court, we were able to find several well known Aussies—including Don Turnbull and Colin

Long, who had played on the Australian Davis Cup team—who gladly agreed to come over and play with us. The courts actually turned out to be very playable.

A special assignment came up in New Guinea. I was selected to handle administrative support for a small group involved in an operation that was probably an early radar outfit, although nothing was said of this highly secretive mission at the time. We were stationed in Nadzab in the Markham Valley, beside a jungle that led down to the sea. I soon learned that a tennis court had been built in that area and that Bitsy Grant, the famous United States Nationals and Davis Cup champion, was stationed nearby with the Fifth Bomber Command. He had been one of America's top players and, though small, was known as a giant-killer. I paid a visit to Bitsy, who said he had no desire to play tennis himself but suggested I call another Atlanta native, a colonel named Nick Powel, who later would achieve tennis fame by writing the code of ethics for tennis. Nick and I played several times. He would call and issue an order saying, "Lieutenant, I'll see you at the court at three o'clock tomorrow," in a somewhat intimidating tone of voice.

Later, when I moved to an isolated spot in the Philippines called Mindoro, Colonel Powel was stationed there as well. A tennis court had been created outside an abandoned sugar mill in such a small space that the cement surface ended at the baseline. This did not keep the colonel and me from playing. One day the heat was so stifling that I thought I would pass out. But I refused to give in, waiting for the colonel to be the first to suggest we quit, which he finally did. Nick Powel ended up back in Washington, and we maintained a strong friendship over the years. We even played together in a Mid-Atlantic Sectional Tennis Tournament and won.

One day in the Philippines while shuffling papers, I noticed that the army in the Asian area was going to pick someone to be sent back to Washington and Lee University for a month-long course in Special Service for Athletics and Recreation. I immediately submitted my application and was selected; and before long I found myself on a plane bound from Manila to Hawaii and then San Francisco. I called Peg and we met in Chicago after being separated for some twenty-seven months.

I had two weeks free before having to report to school, and we were able to return to Washington. When we were there, VE Day was celebrated, which made it increasingly likely that I would never have to return to the Pacific. Nonetheless, I took the course at Washington and Lee, which turned out to be a lot of fun and gave me the opportunity to associate with some of the top athletes and entertainers in the country. When the course ended it was apparent that the war was coming to an end, and I was transferred to Fort Meade, where I was discharged in 1945. For me the war was finally over.

Mary Gregory Ware barber set
Cobalt blue Sandwich Glass vases with amber figures: receptacles for shaving towel (8"x 5 1/2"), and for cologne and water
ARTIST UNKNOWN
circa 1880

CHAPTER 2

Getting Started on a Career

With the end of World War II, the future was wide open. Peg and I wanted to start a family and needed a place to live. My father had decided to move, so we bought his small house in Chevy Chase and undertook some remodeling. I took a couple of night courses at George Washington University School of Law, which I hated. My academic interests were more in the social sciences. So I switched from law to sociology where I enjoyed the coursework. Over the next five years I accumulated enough credits to earn my master's degree. Our first son, Kenneth, was born in 1946, followed by Frank in 1948 and Frederick in 1951. Our daughter Katherine, whom we call Kate, joined us in 1956.

After leaving the army, I was reinstated as a tennis amateur for a brief period due to a one-time dispensation for army personnel who may have had previous tennis teaching experience that prevented them from participating in the major tournaments, which were open only to amateurs. Given the popularity of professional tennis today, it is hard to believe that in those days the real competition was at the amateur level. This, however, was the case. Most tennis professionals earned their living from running clubs and giving lessons rather than from competing for money. There were a few exceptions including Rod Laver, Pancho Gonzalez, Jack Kramer, Bill Tilden, Don Budge, Fred Perry, and Bobby Riggs, who played in matches throughout the country as "touring pros." But those matches, though hard fought and competitive, were considered to be more like exhibitions than like the tennis tournaments we know today. There was no formal organized league or tournament activity for professionals, and only a small number of the very best players participated. Most, like myself, opted for teaching, coaching, and directing tennis club activities.

While I was a graduate student and working at odd jobs, I did take advantage of my new amateur status and entered a couple of tournaments, winning the District of Columbia Championship and getting to the finals in regional competition. But playing amateur tennis and going to graduate school did not put food on the table. I needed a job. When I learned that the Woodmont Country Club, the club where I had previously worked, had a position open for a tennis pro, I jumped at the opportunity.

Woodmont Country Club was situated on land that was soon to be taken over by the United States government for the home of the National Institutes of Health. Part of my job was to help design the layout for the new tennis courts at the new club, a task that I found both challenging and rewarding. Because the new location in surburban Bethesda was remote, part of my job was to promote tennis and to build up a following by having tennis clinics, exhibitions, and tournaments. Before long the interest in tennis became so great that I actually had to put a damper on the promotions so that the facilities would be available for the regular players. But in the early days it was a challenge just to keep the courts full. I drew on the entrepreneurial skills that I had learned from my father, recognizing that only through hard work would the task get done. As part of the promotion effort, we decided on a tennis tournament.

The club agreed to host a tournament but wanted to keep it small. We addressed that concern by making it an invitational event and limiting it only to the top local doubles teams. When I invited the team of Ed Wesley and Harold Freeman, an African American, it created a problem for the club in those days of segregation. I was approached by the club trustees and argued my case strongly. How could a Jewish club be influenced by segregation, which I strongly believed was wrong? The trustees said that they themselves were not against integration but were afraid of what other clubs might say.

I told them that they had no choice and that I would resign before I would withdraw the invitation to Harold Freeman. The trustees finally consented and the tournament was very successful. In 1962, Harold became one of the original members of the St. Albans Tennis Club. He also went on to become a prominent New York physician and to head up the American Cancer Society.

Because in those days tennis activity was relatively slow during certain times of the day, I looked for other opportunities to generate income and learned that Georgetown University was looking for a part-time tennis coach in the afternoons. I took the job in 1953 and worked at Woodmont in the mornings and at Georgetown most afternoons. I fully enjoyed working in the program and I liked the students a great deal, though I was somewhat surprised by the conservatism of many of them. I recall one particular incident in 1954 when the college newspaper asked a group of Georgetown's best students to rank outstanding Americans of the day and Joe McCarthy was their top choice.

GOING ABROAD

At the Woodmont Country Club, I held a tournament for teaching pros. From Harrisburg, Pennsylvania, came a man by the name of Mischa Stahovich, whose family were White Russians who ended up in Austria after fleeing the Communists. Mischa stayed at our house and we had long discussions about life in Europe. Peg and I had wanted to spend time there but had not had an opportunity, and now with three children the expense of going as tourists was beyond our budget.

Mischa volunteered that his old job at the Salzburg Tennis Club was open and suggested that I take the position. I took the dare and requested a year's leave from Woodmont, which was granted. The club gave us a dinner and a set of luggage and we bought tickets on the *Queen Mary*. We set out for Austria, with stops in London and Paris, for our adventure in Europe.

The ship docked in England. Then we went by ferry to the continent, finally arriving by train in the picturesque town of Salzburg in March 1955. We were picked up by the club president in his Volkswagen, the type with the trunk in the front, which we had never seen before. We checked into a small hotel near the train station until we could rent a house. Although it was springtime, it was cold in Austria, and on that day it was raining. In fact, that spring it never seemed to stop raining.

We liked our new house, which was a traditional-style cottage nestled under a hill near a ski lift. The only problem was that with the salary of a tennis pro—paid in Austrian shillings—we had a problem making ends meet.

Lesson time was known as "trainer hour," and I informed my students in English that they were not horses to be trained but students of "the science and art" of tennis. They must learn not just to hit the ball, but also the geometry of tennis, the physics of tennis, and the art of tennis. I felt like a missionary who was teaching them something they had never heard before. My method of teaching, then and now, revolves around the idea that there is a reason for everything you do in tennis. I don't tell anyone on the practice court to do something unless it can be explained, just as you would not want a doctor to give you a pill unless the doctor could tell you what it was supposed to do and why. This is the way that I have always approached tennis, so that my pupils learn the theory and are able to diagnose problems for themselves. My introduction involves a rudimentary knowledge of mathematics, geometry, physics, biology, anatomy, and art, though I will acknowledge that some of the finer points of my lectures may have been missed by many of my Austrian students, whose English was no better than my German.

We had not been in Austria very long when Peg ran into someone with the United States occupation forces who mentioned that there might be a job opening in the recreation department with the United States Army. The idea was appealing. Not only would I get an American salary, paid in dollars, but also the perks of United States dependents, such as schools and commissaries. The new job came through and I started off running the tennis courts at the two U.S. bases in Salzburg and later was involved in setting up ski trips. We made a number of friends, including civilians, refugees, and Austrians who had been my pupils, and we traveled to the lakes and the mountains, to see plays, concerts at the Salzburg Festival, and to play a lot of tennis. In fact, during that time I played in several tournaments in Europe, including the Pro Championship of Holland, where I was able to make it to the finals in doubles competition.

In early 1955 there was rumbling that the four powers, the American, British, French, and the Soviets, were about to leave the occupied land. The mood at the base became more frantic as the deadline approached. Troops were being pulled out, people were being transferred, and equipment was being disposed of quickly. Because I had been hired on the spot, I was not given any great priority and had to find a new job on my own. We could have returned to the United States, but we had planned on staying in Europe for a full year and did not want to pass up that opportunity. The job I was able to land was at the Wheelus Air Force Base in Tripoli, Libya. The thought of a winter on the Mediterranean seemed perfect, so I accepted the position and we headed for Naples, where we boarded a ship for Libya with stops at Siracusa and Malta. On the car ride from the ship to Wheelus, someone mentioned that the base commander was a soccer nut, who believed that soccer should be emphasized as the only true international game. Furthermore, he was on record as saying that there was very little interest in tennis at his base. I did not know a great deal about soccer, but the British troops stationed in the area included well-known soccer players. It was an easy swap. I would give the Brits tennis lessons and they would in turn send their expert soccer players over to coach our troops. Unfortunately, however, except for soccer, little recreation was available on the United States base. In contrast to Europe, where the United States forces furnished their bases with the finest recreational facilities, few such facilities existed in North Africa. Given the heat, the polluted water at the beach, and the dangers for innocent foreigners lurking within the walled city, the military should have provided more for its personnel.

A bus went out from town to Wheelus, passing the market and the fields where the farmers worked with wooden plows. Old people sat on the floor with their eyes blinded by disease caused by flies. The flies were considered sacred because they pollinated the date trees, and for this reason they were not to be removed from a person's eyes. Some families still lived in caves. Life had changed very little for most of the population during the past two thousand years. The country was very poor, and except for the exquisite Roman ruins at Sabratha and Leptis Magna, Libya had little to offer those of us with the military.

While in Libya I received a letter from Woodmont Country Club informing me that although my year's leave of absence entitled me to reapply for the job, the new chairman of the tennis committee did not want to remove his present pro. For this reason the job could not be guaranteed. In short, I did not have a job to go back to. As I look back on it now, this was probably the best thing that could have happened because it pushed me out of what I call the bush league into the majors, and gave me the opportunity to become a tennis entrepreneur.

Even though I no longer had a job waiting for me, Peg and I knew we had to return to Washington. Libya had been interesting, but it really offered no future and did not present any career opportunities. It was not the best environment for our three young sons. Moreover, Peg was pregnant. We knew we had to leave, but we did not know what we were going back to.

Our trip home included a stop in Monte Carlo, where we checked into one of the finest hotels. I was standing in front of the Monte Carlo Country Club, where I would later play and win the senior championships in both the 1980s and 1990s. There I recognized Malcolm Fox, an old friend, who was a strong Baltimore junior player and who played the circuit in Europe for many years as a "tennis bum," earning under-the-table expense money that enabled him to live a rather high lifestyle. I told Malcolm that I didn't have enough money to make the trip home. He pointed out that if I was able to cross the border and cash my dollars into francs I could get the ticket for a lower price, and that is exactly what I did. So we finally boarded the *Roma*, an Italian ship, which was going to sail for the United States from Genoa.

The five of us boarded the ship and soon realized that something was wrong. We didn't have enough blankets and we were unable to get a response when we tried to get through on the phones. The meals were plentiful with pasta and wine but not much more, a far cry from the *Queen Mary*, and not the way to end a beautiful year abroad. When we made the first stop in Naples, I left the ship and went over to the office to tell the company that we wanted to discontinue our voyage and fly home. The company agent was puzzled, not understanding why we weren't happy, until he discovered that we had been placed incorrectly in the lower-class area where the services were minimal. He immediately resolved the situation by moving us up to first class where the rooms were larger and the dining was excellent. The only hitch was that it was March and we encountered extremely rough weather on the Atlantic. Most of the passengers, including Peg and me, spent a large part of the voyage in bed. Our children, who were miraculously spared, ate spaghetti every meal and neglected their showers.

THE SHERATON COURTS

We had leased our home for a year and were able to get it back, but I was faced with the challenge of finding work. As a temporary measure, I started giving tennis lessons on the courts at the old Wardman Park Hotel, which had become the Sheraton Park at the time and now is the Wardman Park Marriott, located off Connecticut Avenue on Woodley Road. This led to my first endeavor as a tennis businessman and was the beginning of a career that I have pursued for some sixty years.

When I found out how much money the hotel was making from the courts, I figured that I could do better if I were running the courts rather than just giving lessons: So in 1955 I proposed to the management that I lease the courts for twice the amount that the hotel was earning from court fees. Naturally they grabbed at the offer. However, I not only doubled their income but also doubled my own by leasing the courts at a slightly higher rate, by increasing court utilization through strong promotion of the sport, and by doing most of the labor myself.

One wing of the Sheraton Park had many high-priced apartments occupied by people well known in Washington. A number of them were regular tennis players, including Chief Justice Earl Warren, who after receiving a death threat was accompanied by a Secret Service agent; Secretary of Defense Neil McElroy; Senator Robert Kerr, the former oil baron from Oklahoma; and Lawrence Spivak, whose TV show *Meet the Press* was the forerunner of today's news talk shows. Many people among the social elite of Washington, such as Bob and Peggy LeBaron, used the court for social purposes, mostly playing with foreign ambassadors, Cabinet-level opponents, and others in local circles.

One resident of the hotel was Sewell Brundage, who in 1961 was on leave from being president of the

Price Waterhouse accounting firm, serving as controller of the currency. His wife, a lovely, gentle pupil of mine, made the suggestion that I call Marg McNamara to see if she would be interested in lessons. I did not call Marg because I did not believe in soliciting business, but she came by to see me. We soon started lessons, which continued for many years until her death several years ago. Her husband, Robert, had recently left the Ford Motor Company to become the secretary of defense in the Kennedy administration and later would head up the World Bank. He also soon became a long-term tennis pupil and a friend for more than forty years.

The Sheraton courts attracted outsiders as well, including columnist Walter Lippmann, General Telford Taylor of the Nuremberg trials, General Alfred Grunther, the World War II hero, Senator Ernest Gruening from Alaska, and Dr. Janet Travell, President Kennedy's doctor. It was truly a lively place in those days.

To help promote the courts, I organized several exhibitions. One brought in Roy Emerson and Neal Frasier from Australia, two top Davis Cup players, who played against Vic Seixas and Hamilton Richardson, Davis Cup players for the United States team. In the late 1950s I staged a rematch of the famous match between Althea Gibson, the premier player of the day and an African American, and Shirley Fry, a Wimbledon finalist in the mid-1950s. In his radio program, Edward P. Morgan commented on this exhibition, saying that until very recently segregation had not permitted such events to occur in Washington. One of the most enthusiastic fans at that match was Chief Justice Earl Warren, who had presided over the recent Supreme Court decision *Brown* v. *Board of Education.*

GOODWILL AMBASSADOR

The courts at Sheraton Park had the Har-Tru fast-drying clay surface, and because they were in a shady place, they were always in great shape. But because Washington winters are somewhat unpredictable, the courts had to close when the first frost appeared. This meant I did not have a job during the winter months. In 1957 that turned out not to be a problem when I was asked by the State Department to serve on a special assignment in Haiti.

Back in those days, the word "diplomat" conjured up for me the image of a stodgy WASP male in formal dress with a fake accent. I was in for a surprise when I met the officers of the Department of State division known as the International Educational Exchange Service. This program had sent performing artists and athletes such as Maria Tallchief, Louis Armstrong, and Benny Goodman to foreign countries as goodwill ambassadors. I was the first tennis professional to be given this honor and was posted to Haiti for six months, just four weeks after our daughter Kate was born.

I went to Haiti in the fall of 1957. Peg and the children followed several weeks later. I arrived at the Port au Prince airport and, after being pushed ahead of everyone, was waved through customs and driven to the Bellevue Club where I was to work. The rule in the tropics, I was told, was that no one was supposed to drink before sundown. Accordingly, my genial host waited until the sun was setting and then began pushing rum and sodas at me. We had consumed a fair number when someone suggested that we play tennis. I never was too enthusiastic about playing under artificial lights, and those lights were horrible. Between the poor lighting and the effects of the rum and soda, my performance was not up to par. In fact, the next day I had trouble remembering my performance at all. I am surprised the State Department didn't send me back on the next plane.

The object of the tour was to spread good will through cultural exchange. Haiti, of course, was, and still is, one of the poorest countries in the world. At the time it was ripe for revolution. Developing a better understanding through exchange programs was new to Haiti and most of those participating were from the upper classes and were leaders of the country. Even so, while some of the people whom I taught or coached could afford to pay for their lessons, they were the minority and they did not pay very much.

I taught at two of the clubs in Port au Prince, but I also went down to the local courts next to the stadium to give clinics to people who could not afford to pay. We worked out a program that included lessons, tournaments, a Junior Davis Cup squad, and exhibitions. The program was popular and generated a lot of enthusiasm. In addition to tennis, Peg and I attended a number of parties and invited people to our home, trying to establish as much "good will" as we could.

The greatest challenge to this cultural exchange actually came from the diplomatic community, which was very set in its old conservative ways. This community had its own racially segregated club, which the locals despised, even though many of the Haitians were actually educated in Europe and Canada. The club members asked me if I would give them lessons at their own club. I told them that that was not why I was in Haiti, but if they wanted a tennis lesson, they could make arrangements to take one at one of the Haitian clubs where I was teaching. While most did not take me up on the offer, a handful did, which pleased the Haitians.

The tennis program in Haiti was a microcosm of social conditions in other areas of the society. I was supposedly working for the United States government, but the State Department workers in Haiti practiced segregation and did not wish to cooperate with me on my program. They saw this as an unorthodox method of diplomacy, which was a threat to them. On the other hand, the Haitians loved the program and immediately took Peg and me into their social network. We socialized with Haitians at all levels, including the leaders of the country as well as ordinary citizens. We had a large party once where the few Americans who came were amazed at the number and the "importance" of the guests who attended. They were professionals, businessmen, and military and government leaders. Most spoke English, as did their children, though they would throw in a lot of *patois* when talking among themselves.

Despite the unorthodox nature of the program, it was heralded by many in the State Department as a great success. The junior program eventually sent several boys to United States colleges, and the Junior Davis Cup team was established with a real Davis Cup being awarded, thanks to United States Ambassador Roy Tasco Davis.

The Haitians were experiencing a series of uprisings when we were getting ready to leave. One event was especially emotional. As a passive show of strength, all the businesses shut down, and people marched in a silent parade to show their unity in opposition to the government headed by Paul Magloire. For the first time in memory, the Mardi Gras ball at the Bellevue Club was not held. In fact, the lights stayed off until just before we left, when they were turned back on in my honor as the Tennis Association hosted a large party for me and my family, presenting me with a carved wooden Haitian head, which they said symbolized our return to Haiti some day.

The tennis program in Haiti actually became something of a controversy in Washington when Congressman John Rooney from Brooklyn, who was always looking for ways to cut the federal budget, saw a notice that I would be returning to Washington after this tour of Haiti and immediately branded the program an irresponsible allocation of United States dollars. He questioned the value of a tennis program in a third world country and provoked a debate on the floor of the House over this issue. Congressman Walter Judd from Minnesota made an impassioned speech spelling out my qualifications, declaring that if we wanted to fight Communism in the world we needed more Allie Ritzenbergs.

Several years later, my friend Libby Rowe wanted to get Congressman Fred Rooney into the St. Albans Tennis Club. She pointed out to me that he was the congressman from Pennsylvania, not New York, adding, "He is the good Rooney."

TENNIS ENTREPRENEUR

In those days, the only indoor courts in Washington belonged to a few private organizations and were not open to nonmembers. Congressional Country Club had one indoor court. Another was located on the second floor of a building in downtown Washington, and a third court was at Bolling Air Force Base in southwest Washington. I thought this dearth presented an opportunity for a business venture, so in 1960 I rented the second floor of a garage next to an apartment complex called Pooks Hill. This was on the old estate of Princess Martha of Norway, best known for President Roosevelt's weekend visits to play cards during World War II and long since demolished. Unfortunately, the courts did not reflect those high-class origins. The playing surface was concrete. The ceilings were very low, only twenty-four feet, and the back court was dangerously short. In spite of these conditions, we made do, and I was able to attract enough venturesome players so that the venture was viable. Dr. Janet Travell, the White House physician for President Kennedy, and Tish Baldridge, the White House social secretary, were both regular players.

Shortly after I opened this court my landlord decided to build a new apartment complex, with an indoor tennis facility. So I closed the Pooks Hill court and helped to start the Linden Hill club. My old customers switched over to play on the new courts, which were built with the soft green Har-Tru clay surface in keeping with the luxury club image that the owners wanted to project. The problem was that Har-Tru courts required a lot of water to be in prime shape; otherwise the surface became hard, dusty, and very difficult for tennis shoes to grip. Watering the courts indoors, however, produced strong humidity and condensation and created a Turkish bath atmosphere, which wreaked havoc with the well-coiffed hair of the women players of the day.

I decided not to stay at Linden Hill and started looking for another site. When I heard that the Marriott Corporation was going to close down its warehouse at its national headquarters on River Road in Bethesda, within walking distance of the D.C. line, I leased the building and converted the dilapidated structure into a suitable place for two courts. Before Marriott used the building for a warehouse, it had been used for cutting stone for the Washington National Cathedral. It had high, inaccessible windows, several of which had been shattered, allowing easy access for pigeons and occasional raccoons, which could be spotted moving slowly along the iron rafters.

We created two mini locker rooms out of walk-in refrigerators, improved the lighting, painted the walls, and scrubbed down the grease-stained floor, but we needed a new surface to make the courts attractive and playable. A few years earlier the Astrodome in Houston had introduced the world to Astroturf, which at the time seemed the perfect solution. My courts were the first indoor Astroturf tennis courts; and for all I know, they may have been the last. The carpet installers did a fine job, but they clearly had never painted stripes on tennis courts, as they extended the service line all the way back to the baseline, an action we had to correct as best we could.

A friend, Tury Herndon, volunteered to decorate the place. On the locker walls she painted a Monopoly board with the toilet marked as "Jail." She plunked secondhand sofas in each locker room and a few brightly colored Adirondack chairs in the small alcove entrance next to the loading dock doors. Our landlord was the company's founder, Willard Marriott, who would later brag about having tennis courts at the corporate headquarters. He liked to take visitors on tour and show them the makeshift tennis center where an abandoned crane stood between courts one and two.

Because many of the players who played on the court were among Washington's elite, Maxine Cheshire, a gossip columnist for *The Washington Post,* would often call me to get tidbits about them. Not wanting to interfere with their privacy, I usually abstained from giving her any specific information; but on one occasion I made an exception. I called Maxine and said that I had something interesting that only she could write about. I told her that the news was that some of the Washington women who had been playing at the humid courts at Linden Hill struggled to find ways to combat the hair problem caused by the excessive moisture. Joan Kennedy often wore a bandanna, Lydia Katzenbach, wife of the assistant attorney general, Nick Katzenbach, wore a shower cap, and Marg McNamara donned a hat. But now that they had moved to my indoor courts on River Road, their hair no longer needed protection and they were pleased. The article appeared in *The Washington Post,* and within days my courts were completely sold out.

To lighten the load on our tiny staff, I gave all the players a key to the building so they could enter for their assigned times on their own. That system did have a few drawbacks. For example, we stayed open until midnight. Since the eleven o'clock hour was somewhat difficult to sell, I devised a bargain price for those who wanted to take the last two hours from 10:00 to 12:00. Ellen Proxmire, wife of the Wisconsin senator, had the ten o'clock hour for one night a week but refused to reserve the additional hour at half price. No problem, I told her, and then promptly sold the second hour to someone else. Ellen was livid. How could I do this to her, she exclaimed. Actually, I was aware that some of the players would routinely play beyond their allotted times and that did not bother me. I was more concerned about reports that some players would continue playing well into the wee hours of the morning.

I kept the River Road tennis facility open until about 1980, by which time a number of other better facilities had sprouted up around the area, and the charm of the old building no longer had the drawing power to attract regular players. The facility maintained a small but devoted clientele and stayed open for several more years, run by Val Lubbers, who also has been my assistant for many years at the St. Albans Tennis Club.

PAULINE BETZ ADDIE

In addition to running the River Road facility, I also was involved in running the tennis center in Cabin John, Maryland. Pauline Betz, for years one of the best women players in the country, was one of my two partners.

I was especially lucky to have Pauline as a partner. She was indeed quite a personality. She had appeared on the cover of *Life* magazine, her flaming red hair aglow; and she had led a glamorous life, dating Hollywood's most eligible men and consorting with the rich and famous. On the tennis courts, she moved like a gazelle. Her backhand was patterned after Don Budge's, a truly remarkable shot, and it was no wonder that Pauline Betz had won the United States Women's championship four times at Forest Hills (1942, 1943, 1944, and 1946).

Pauline's mother, Betsy, taught physical education in the California school system and was quite a good athlete herself. Both mother and daughter were also excellent bridge players. They both played as masters in the top bridge tournaments. Once during a break between bridge sessions, Pauline went out to the tennis courts of the hotel and proceeded to overpower the local pro. Her mother was sitting on the sidelines when another spectator marveled at how well this woman was playing. He turned to Pauline's mother and asked if her daughter had ever considered playing competitively. Betsy replied, "Oh, well, she did win Wimbledon once, but then she only played it once."

After the United States Lawn Tennis Association barred Pauline from playing amateur tennis, she joined the tour with Jack Kramer, where she played against "Gorgeous Gussy" Moran in a lopsided series. Pauline later admitted to Jack Kramer that she should have eased up and made it look a little closer. Playing in her leopard skin designer shorts, she was not only the best tennis player, she was the most attractive one as well.

Pauline later married Bob Addie, a Washington sports writer of the old school, who specialized in covering baseball.

I was always trying to create interest through exhibitions. Pauline was cooperative and we would often play, thankful for even a meager turnout. In 1954, we played at Georgetown University where she showed up in shorts, a violation of the school's policy, which prohibited all women from playing on the courts without "proper tennis attire." On that occasion, however, no one said a word, and the university president, a Jesuit priest, presented Pauline with a huge bouquet of flowers at the end of the tennis match.

As operators of the Cabin John Indoor Tennis Center, we took on tasks that many new employees would never stoop to do. If the ice and snow flooded the courts, Pauline and I mopped the floor. On one such occasion on our hands and knees, I turned to Pauline and remarked, "You won Wimbledon and I am the president of a corporation. Look where we ended up."

Pauline loved to keep busy, which made her a wonderful business partner. She handled most of the paper work. The contrast between her and the present champions is remarkable. Now players at the top are one dimensional, with tennis often the only ingredient in their lives. Pauline, on the other hand, earned a graduate degree in economics while playing serious tennis. In addition to tennis and bridge, she was a fine musician, played numerous instruments, and was an accomplished linguist. She won speed typing contests, qualified for the Olympics in track and field, played table tennis exhibitions, shot par golf, and learned to operate a computer at remarkable speed. Yet when she and I worked together at the Tennis Center, we had no pictures of her on the walls. In fact, most people were not even aware of her background or accomplishments.

Her success bolsters my theory that champions have an inherent drive that overcomes all obstacles. They seem to have a built-in need and drive to succeed. There was once an old saying about the best athlete being a hungry athlete. Most great athletes seem to have a fire in the belly causing a hunger that drives them to achieve excellence. Pauline was certainly one of these people.

THE CABIN JOHN COURTS

In the Cabin John enterprise, which began in 1961 and lasted through 1981, Stanley Hoffberger was the third partner. He was outstanding in finance. The Cabin John indoor courts turned out to be a huge success. The Maryland National Park and Planning Commission wanted to open an indoor tennis facility, but they were short of funds, so to accomplish the task they put the plan out for bid. We were the successful bidders and set out to build a six-court complex on the park property. Though financing was not easy, we were able to get a loan, which both Pauline and I signed with our spouses, guaranteeing the bank against any losses. Thus, if the project failed, our homes and assets were on the line. Because Stanley's wife, Judy, was heir to a huge fortune, her lawyers would not permit her to be liable. This appeared strange to me—that the people who actually had the money would not sign—but Stan did shoulder a good portion of the initial construction loan and the project got underway. The lease ultimately ran for twenty-one years with the Park and Planning Agency receiving a percentage of gross, approving the rates, and acquiring the building at the expiration of the lease. It turned out to be a good deal for the government, though we probably would have been much better off had we acquired some land and built and owned the structure ourselves. But we loved the work and earned reasonable revenues from the enterprise.

RICHARD PANCHO GONZALEZ

In the fall of 1962, just after I had started the St. Albans Tennis Club, I got a call from Tish Baldridge asking,

"How would you like to have Pancho Gonzalez for a week?" At the time Pancho Gonzalez was one of the most famous tennis players in the world. He was in his mid-30s and still close to his prime. Naturally, I wanted to know what was the catch.

Tish said that because he was in a contract dispute with Jack Kramer, to whom he was under contract, he could not give any tennis exhibitions for money. But he was also on the payroll of Huntington Hartford as the resident pro at Paradise Island in the Bahamas. In an effort to show good will to President Kennedy, Hartford offered to let Gonzalez come to Washington and offer his services at no cost. This way Gonzalez did not run into trouble with Kramer. So Gerald Wagner, a public relations guru who represented a number of New York companies, and his wife, who was the fashion editor of *The Washington Post,* coordinated the event.

Wagner arranged for Gonzalez, who preferred to be called Richard rather than Pancho, and his wife Madeleine and their two newborn twins, to stay in one of Washington's most fashionable new apartment houses. I was to be their host. So what was I going to do with this charismatic tennis genius?

With the help of Tish and Jerry, I mapped out a tentative schedule. Shortly after arriving, Gonzalez said that he needed some dress shirts and asked if I could take him to a store specializing in quality clothing. I decided to take him to Lewis & Thomas Saltz, which at the time was considered Washington's premier men's shop. After surveying us and sizing up Gonzalez the salesman took out a box and offered the shirts, to which Gonzalez politely asked, "Don't you have anything better?" He finally settled on several of the store's best shirts.

That week was "Gonzalez week" at the Ritzenbergs. We invited him to our house, where he seemed to enjoy playing with our children. The next day I sent him up to Capitol Hill to have lunch with Claiborne Pell, the senator from Rhode Island. Claiborne's relative was a member of the Newport Tennis Hall of Fame, and his wife, Nuala, was related to Huntington Hartford. The next night we asked Ambassador B. K. Nehru, from India, to host a cocktail party with Gonzalez as the honored guest. This also turned out to be a magnificent event.

The next day we took Gonzalez to Mt. Vernon, and on the way back we stopped at the home of Supreme Court Justice Hugo Black, who was also a tennis enthusiast. Originally we were going to play tennis with the judge, but a recent medical exam had shown something that caused his doctor to forbid Justice Black from playing tennis until additional tests could be made. Black had an old historic home in Alexandria, Virginia. In the rear, he had a clay court, which he rolled daily with a hand-pushed heavy roller. He liked the game so much that when he married his second wife, Elizabeth, he sent her out for tennis lessons the following day. Black had been a controversial figure earlier in his career but had radically changed his opinions, becoming more liberal, and I found him to be a truly fascinating person. Gonzalez enjoyed meeting the judge but we were all disappointed not to be able to play tennis.

A major part of Gonzalez's stay, of course, involved the tennis exhibitions. Pauline Betz Addie agreed to play along with me and the Japanese ambassador. The first exhibition was on behalf of the children of Junior Village, a home for orphaned and abandoned children and one of Jackie Kennedy's favorite charities. It rained on the scheduled day, and I was later told by one of the diplomats working at the Japanese embassy that the ambassador spent most of the day peering out of the window, not knowing whether to be sad or glad.

Although that exhibition was postponed, we were able to put together a match involving Gar Mulloy, a former United States Amateur and Wimbledon doubles champion, who happened to be in Washington for a promotional event. He happily accepted the invitation to play with Gonzalez, Pauline, and me. Gar and I teamed up against Pauline and Gonzalez.

During that game Gonzalez played brilliantly, and at one point in the match, to the delight of the crowd, he retrieved a ball from a ledge that my youngest son Fred, the ball boy, could not reach. Gonzalez reached up and grabbed the ball, then handed it to Fred, who in turn gave it back to him for the serve. This gesture got a lot of laughs from the enthusiastic crowd.

My daughter, Kate, was only six years old at the time, but she was intrigued by this gentle giant. In fact, she exclaimed that she would never wash the hand that Gonzalez had grasped when shaking hands with her.

During the visit, the four of us, Pauline, Gar, Gonzalez, and I, took a trip out to Bethesda Naval Hospital, where I had a conversation with one of the research doctors, who had examined Gonzalez at a previous time. He told me that Gonzalez had the largest lung capacity of any individual he had ever studied.

The final tennis exhibition was on the sprawling grounds of St. Elizabeth's Hospital, the largest mental institution in the country and known at the time as an "insane asylum." This was an informal show where we involved people with little tennis experience. One of the participants I took along was a man named Win Webber, a person I knew who had barely been able to get out of a cab two years earlier, when he could hardly stand, much less run. Win was about seventy-five years old and had been a patient at St. Elizabeth's himself, which I thought made him an ideal candidate for the exhibition. He had recently started taking lessons from me and playing tennis again, having played competitive tennis years earlier as a member of the Dartmouth College tennis team. He enthusiastically joined in the game. We also brought along with us Bo Jones, who was then eighteen and the junior champion of Washington, and one day would become the publisher of *The Washington Post.* One of the patients of the institution who got to hit with Gonzalez was so excited after playing that I was later told doctors had to resort to severe measures to calm him down after the experience.

After the tennis clinic, we were invited to the residence of the superintendent of St. Elizabeth's for refreshments. When I introduced Win Webber to the doctor, I casually mentioned that he was an alumnus of the institution, a statement that the doctor did not seem to comprehend. But later, after Webber had contacted the doctor to get his medical records, the superintendent called me to say that Win's recovery had been absolutely miraculous. When he arrived at the hospital, he was in such a poor state of physical and mental health that the doctors had very little hope for his recovery. That he would be playing an exhibition match with one of the greatest tennis players of all time was almost incomprehensible.

During the week that Richard "Pancho" Gonzalez was in Washington, he seemed to enjoy himself greatly. He mixed with the spectators and was in no way the grouchy person that he had been portrayed by the press to be. Before he left town, we arranged for a tour of the White House. Six of us, the Gonzalezes, the Wagners, and the Ritzenbergs, piled into Jerry Wagner's old Bentley and headed to the White House. Jerry was driving, and as we reached the gate the guards asked him to show his identification. Of all the times to forget one's wallet, this had to be one of the worst; but

Jerry did not have his. Fortunately the guards recognized me because at the time I was giving tennis lessons to the First Lady, so we were able to get in.

After we entered, we peered out of a window and noticed that President Kennedy was conducting a swearing in ceremony in the Rose Garden. We turned our attention to viewing the items on the wall in the Cabinet Room, and I turned to Peggy and said, "Do you think the president will come in?" As she was answering "no," Tish Baldridge, his social secretary and also a good friend of mine, left the room and suddenly reappeared with the president. He was in a jovial mood and wanted to discuss tennis, asking us about the relatively new sensation, Rod Laver. His Boston accent made it sound like "Lahver." He then left us, only to return moments later to rejoin us and talk more about tennis. The time with Jack Kennedy surely was one of the highlights of the week for Gonzalez, and for all of us.

Not long after that experience Gonzalez was able to have the restriction of playing only for Kramer lifted. He agreed to play in a tournament that I was running at Cole Field House, the University of Maryland's indoor stadium. Rod Laver, Lew Hoad, and many of the greats of that period were entered. Prior to the start, we had a kickoff lawn party at my home in Bethesda. By this time, Gonzalez had separated from his wife, Madeleine, and was going with a TV actress. He had missed the plane with the troupe of players, who were grumbling about the situation. When he finally arrived at the party with his new woman friend, he was in a pretty bad mood. Unlike the week that he spent with us before, he practically ignored my children, a situation they found somewhat disillusioning.

The last time I saw Gonzalez was a number of years later in the mid-1970s, when he was playing in a Grand Masters tour event in Aspen, Colorado. The high altitude where breathing is labored and tennis balls often sail uncontrollably made playing tennis very difficult. Gonzalez was not playing well and lost the match. He complained about a number of line calls. He was also in a pretty bad emotional state as he stalked off the courts. I decided not to try to talk to him, because everybody who knew him knew that it was best to avoid him when he was in one of his notorious bad moods. I never saw him again and still regret that I missed the chance to talk to him then.

His death in 1997 created a real void in tennis. Bobby Riggs and Richard "Pancho" Gonzalez—perhaps the two most charismatic players in tennis history—died that same year. Richard had come a long way from the Mexican-American neighborhood in Los Angeles where he grew up and had fought discrimination to become one of the most admired tennis players in the world. He could be a most charming individual, with his big smile and warm personality, or he could intimidate everyone when he became angry. His superb athletic ability, however, was undeniable. He was an aggressive tennis player with his big serve, but he was also great defensively because of his quickness and speed. His gracefulness was like that of a cat, appreciated by both tennis experts and the general public alike.

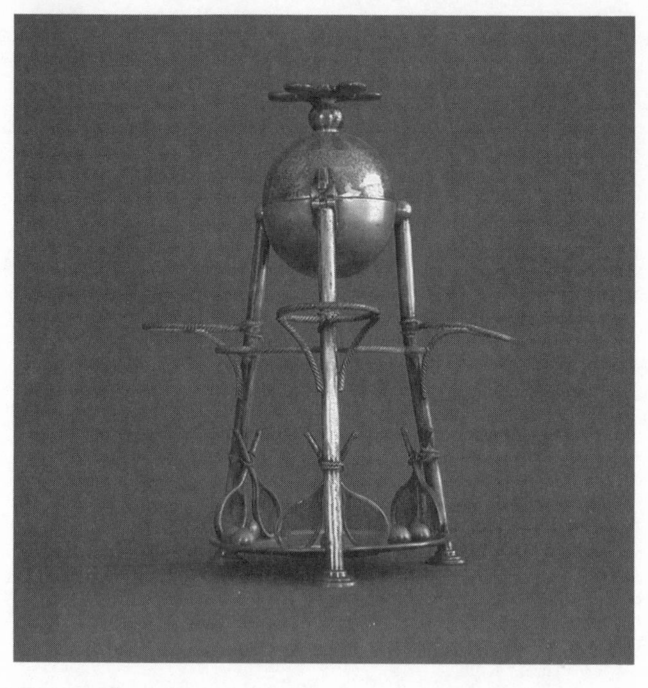

Lemonade maker
circa 1890 10" x 6" x 6"

CHAPTER 3

Launching the St. Albans Tennis Club

While at the Sheraton I had given lessons to members of the Symington family. Lloyd Symington was very involved with St. Albans School and with the National Cathedral. On several occasions he had asked me if I would be interested in taking the job as tennis coach of St. Albans School. My response—which was half serious—was that they could not afford me.

St. Albans School for Boys, located adjacent to the National Cathedral, had then, as it does now, a reputation for providing a rigorous academic program for grades four through twelve. The school's tennis courts, with slow drying sandy clay surfaces, had fallen into disrepair and were almost unplayable. In 1962, the administration was looking for someone to take charge of a school tennis program and to coach at all levels. St. Albans was well located, close enough to downtown to attract people who might want to play before or after work; and it had a reputation as one of Washington's elite private schools. The setting was also beautiful. You could play tennis and look up at the giant towers of the Cathedral, and at nearby football, baseball, and soccer fields. When athletic events were happening in these areas, the atmosphere felt active and vital. The school definitely had potential as a site for a new tennis club.

The job involved starting up a new tennis club to generate revenue to pay off the costs of necessary court renovations, and the upkeep and maintenance of the new courts. A tennis club already existed, but it was small and charged only $15 to $25 for summer membership.

I was somewhat cool to the idea when Lloyd first mentioned it, but when I realized that the Sheraton courts would be closing down to make room for the expansion of the hotel, suddenly the proposal became very appealing. Though I was anxious about the challenges of starting a new club from scratch, the timing could not have been better. Not only did this answer the question of where I would go next, but the closing of the Sheraton meant we had an initial, ready-made market of displaced tennis players to draw on.

The most appealing aspect of the proposal was that I would largely be given free reign to run the club the way I wanted, provided I also met the needs of the students. Lloyd suggested a meeting with the headmaster of St. Albans School, Canon Charles Martin, and we immediately hit it off. I think Canon Martin had made up his mind ahead of time that I was the right person for the job; by the time of the interview, there was no need for persuasion. I was already convinced that this was the right thing for me to do. So I jumped at the opportunity.

Starting up a new tennis club is always a challenge, but given the circumstances, I did not think recruiting new members would be difficult. Canon Martin suggested that the club should give priority to alumni and parents of the school. They would represent about one-third of the total membership. My job was to recruit the other two-thirds.

My friend and pupil Tish Baldridge played at the Sheraton Park courts where I was the professional. She agreed to help me with recruitment. A number of people already playing on the St. Albans courts agreed to sign up, though they complained about the big jump in fees from $25 a season to $75 a season ($150 for families). And naturally we decided to go after the soon-to-be-displaced Sheraton players. Tish and I came up with a list of names of Sheraton players who might be interested. While the process was informal, the tennis grapevine soon took over and enthusiasm began to build. We also focused our efforts on the Kennedy administration because Tish knew a lot of people and tennis was generally preferred over golf. The price of the club was relatively low by the standards of the day, and the courts were not located very far from the Sheraton or from the White House. Furthermore, other opportunities for tennis in Washington were limited at that time.

In setting up the new club, we first had to come up with some operating procedures. My goal was to keep the club as low-key and informal as possible. The most important rule had to do with signing in and limiting the number of guests. There would be no reservations, but players would have to sign in and should not be able to sign in until at least two people were present. Guest fees were modest, and in a given season after a guest had used the courts three times, the players were subject to being bumped by another member who was waiting for a court. Though I have never really considered myself a traditionalist, I also encouraged members to wear whites. Though I realize that the tennis dress code has changed over the years, wearing whites for me represents the grand history of the game and is one tradition that I have not been willing to let go of.

I had one other very strong preference: the club should be racially integrated. This was a bedrock issue for me and I think it contributed in part to why the courts attracted the kind of membership that it did. Many of the people coming into Washington as part of the Kennedy administration were tennis players and they were looking for a good place to play, but they were also sensitive to the issue of racial segregation and they did not want to belong to clubs and organizations that excluded African Americans, as was the case in those days with many of the country clubs in Washington. The St. Albans courts offered them a perfect outlet where the tennis program was just as strong as that of any of the country clubs and where they could feel comfortable with their values.

Our hard work paid off. The initial members of the club included Tish Baldridge, Bob and Marg McNamara, Mary and McGeorge Bundy, Walt Rostow, Arthur and Marion Schlesinger, Phyllis and Douglas Dillon, Jacob Javits, Claiborne Pell, Janet Travell and her husband, John Powell, Carl and Vivien Rowan, and Mike Feldman, among others. These people gave the club instant credibility. The full directory of members for 1962 is included in the appendix.

GETTING INTO THE ST. ALBANS TENNIS CLUB

Club membership in the new St. Albans Tennis Club grew quickly, and within a year we had a waiting list. This meant that getting into the club became an issue. A special committee was set up—actually a committee of one and that was me—to determine who would be accepted as member. While "the committee" has generally followed a policy of first-come-first-served, over the years it has made some exceptions.

We have been true to the requirement stipulated by Canon Martin to give priority to parents and friends of the school, and we have expanded that circle to include people who have made an exceptional contribution to the community. If someone gives up an important position to come to Washington, for example, and contributes to public service, the committee has tended to look kindly on that person. If another individual is running for president of the United States, or some other high office, we make room for that person. When we are approached by a donor to a major art gallery or a museum, who has given a lot to the city, we usually will find a membership spot. These priorities, while important, have accounted for no more than about 25 percent of new members. The rest are taken as their names come up on the waiting list.

However, the membership policies have created a rather ticklish problem and left open the door for lobbying by various members to get their friends included. Some members routinely like to show their influence and volunteer to help an applicant by calling or sending recommendations and writing letters. Sometimes the letters help. More often they don't. It depends on the sender. On more than one occasion, important personalities have bombarded my office with recommendations that usually include the phrase "So-and-So will be a great asset to the club." A director of the CIA once sent me a letter recommending a new member. When I saw the director, I asked him how important it was to him. Was he just being accommodating, or did he really want to see the person in the club? As I suspected, it was of no great importance, so that applicant went on the waiting list. Another applicant sent me a picture of himself with then-President Ronald Reagan to enhance his stature. That was not good enough. Six years later, at the urgent request of a member who was highly regarded, the committee finally let him in. It turned out that our original appraisal had been correct. He continually made poor line calls in his own favor, was pushy, and had a generally unpleasant personality.

Joe Califano urgently called one day when he was secretary of what was then the Department of Health, Education and Welfare requesting membership for a potential employee. This man was an expert on health insurance and did not want to leave his tennis in California to come to Washington unless he could get into a good tennis club. I felt this was the least I could do for my country and found a place for him. The appointee came to town, played tennis frequently and enjoyed his stay. Unfortunately, friction developed between him and Joe and he soon left his post, though he did stay in Washington and continued playing tennis at the club for a number of years.

While playing a senior tournament in Las Vegas once, I had several messages to call the vice president,

Fritz [Walter] Mondale. Thinking the matter was urgent, I immediately returned the call, as Fritz was a good friend and one of my pupils. Mondale apologized, saying he hadn't realized that I was out of town and had only wanted me to consider for membership one of the governors of the Federal Reserve Board.

When John Heinz was a senator, he sent a humorous note requesting membership for his friend and classmate, Congressman Tim Wirth, who was later to become a senator from Colorado. Tim was in the middle of a difficult reelection campaign against an opponent strongly backed by the ultraconservative Coors family. I picked up the phone, called Wirth and said that anyone on the Coors' hit list could get into the St. Albans Tennis Club, no questions asked. Overhearing the phone call, Daniel Schorr, the newscaster who at the time was on President Richard Nixon's so-called "enemies list," muttered that he was on a lot more hit lists than Tim Wirth. In fact, a good number of people playing tennis at the club were probably on Nixon's and other conservatives' enemies list.

On one occasion I got a call from the publisher of *The Washington Post*, Katherine Graham. I could tell by her tone of voice that she was anxious. She started off with, "Allie, in all these years, have I ever asked you for a favor?" She seemed to be getting more uncomfortable as she repeated the question.

"No, Kay," I replied, "but I'd be happy to help if I can."

She then said that a certain person in town was anxious to get into the club and wondered if I could help. After I had gotten her settled down by telling her it would be taken care of, she exclaimed, "Allie, why is it so important to get into the fucking club?"

I told her son, Don, when I saw him on the courts that his mother had been spending too much time around Ben Bradlee.

Some people have argued that Democrats have a better chance of getting into the club than Republicans. While it is true that Democrats have outnumbered Republicans by a significant margin—and while it is also true that I was listed as the coach of the Democratic group when they were playing the Republicans in a tennis tournament at what is now the site of the Fitzgerald Tennis Center in Washington—Republicans do have a chance of getting in and are not excluded just because of their partisan affiliation. In fact, a number of excellent Republicans have been members of the club, including Jacob Javits, Mac Mathias, John Lindsay, Red Blount, James Buckley, Lamar Alexander, the first George Bush, Bill Webster, Gail Wilensky, Michael Boskin, Douglas Dillon, Bill Scranton, Bill Seidman, Bill Frist, John Heinz, Howard Baker, John Warner, and Larry Pressler, among others.

One ticklish situation occurred when a former cabinet officer applied for membership in St. Albans. He also had been the head of the National Association of Manufacturers, which had led the fight to derail Bill

Lubbers' pending appointment as general counsel for the National Labor Relations Board. Republicans felt that Lubbers was too liberal and they wanted someone more sympathetic to business. But Val Lubbers, Bill's wife, has worked in our tennis office for many years and all the paperwork dealing with new members has to cross her desk. This applicant did not make it in.

At President Bill Clinton's sports award dinner in 1993, I was accompanied by my daughter, Kate, because Peg was traveling. It was an unusual event with the Nike corporation picking up the huge tab at which President Clinton was to honor Arthur Ashe by giving a posthumous Medal of Freedom to Ashe's widow.* Kate and I had front row seats within reaching distance of the president. The late Don Budge and his wife were sitting on our right and Colin Powell and his family on our left. Behind us was Vernon Jordan, whose first remark to me was, "Allie, I hope you can get Ken Brody into the club. He is coming down to head up the Export Import Bank." I replied, "It's already taken care of, Vernon."

When Canon Martin, the revered headmaster of St. Albans during the early years of the program, was questioned about membership in the tennis club, he would typically answer, "It's easier to get into the gates of heaven than it is to get into the St. Albans Tennis

*Others honored that evening included Muhammad Ali, Kareem Abdul-Jabbar, Arnold Palmer, Wilma Rudolph, and Ted Williams.

Club. Allie Ritzenberg runs it and I don't interfere." One day, however, Canon Martin's office sent an urgent message that he would like to see two people admitted to the club. Without hesitation, I invited them to join, and they turned out to be fine individuals. Some years later I learned that the Cathedral had had financial difficulties. If it could not raise a substantial amount of money quickly, the scaffolding for some construction would have to be taken down, greatly increasing the project's cost. The two new members, David Busby and Ronald Petri, had negotiated a multimillion dollar loan to save the day. I was happy to help them. They were never aware until much later that they alone had been singled out by Charlie Martin.

THE GANG OF EIGHT

When the St. Albans Tennis Club renewal letter goes out each year to the membership, it contains a sentence reading, "I am familiar with the rules, and family members are aware of them, also." Members sign and return the forms. At the courts members must sign in. From time to time players will forge signatures so they can get on the court even though their partner has not yet arrived. A high percentage of signatures are illegible. Nor is it rare for people to record starting at a later time in order to play longer. Upon occasion, some have refused to get off the court when their playing time has expired. On the whole, however, the system has worked effectively and has served the club and its members well.

Signing in, however, was a perennial problem for one group. They referred to themselves as the "Gang of Eight," although more than that number of people were involved. They had two doubles games starting at 7:00 A.M. on Wednesdays and Fridays. The players tended to come early. We didn't allow players to start before 6:45 A.M., so as not to disturb families living in the homes opposite the courts.

The Gang of Eight would usually start off with the first two players taking the court and the next two taking a second court, since 7:00 A.M. was a busy hour and the courts were always in demand at that time. As the courts were secured, the next four players would fill in. Because the Gang was composed of more than eight, a simplified schedule was made and sent to the homes and offices of these people. But invariably, either seven or nine players showed up. To deal with that problem, they adopted the system of having the first four players take a court and letting the remainder fend for themselves. This tended to create confusion for them and others. Someone in the Gang of Eight once commented, "It's the *Miracle on 34th Street* when we just get eight players," referring to the classic Christmas movie and the fact that the courts are located at the intersection of 34th and Garfield Streets. Jimmy Symington often took the blame for the confusion among the Gang of Eight. However, Jim, a former congressman from Missouri and State Department chief of protocol, was a person of such talent, charm, and decency that no one could ever be annoyed at him, even if he was the culprit.

THE CLUB MEMBERS

One of my first pupils was Marg McNamara, who had started lessons with me at the Sheraton almost from the day she came to Washington in 1961. After I moved to St. Albans she wanted to get her husband, Bob, who was then the secretary of defense in the Kennedy administration, to play tennis; but he was embarrassed to play where he would be seen. By playing squash with Orville Freeman, the former secretary of agriculture and governor of Minnesota, he could play unseen within the confines of a walled court. When Orville went on vacation, Marg approached her husband about taking lessons from me. In those early years, most people played at 7:30 A.M. and then rushed off to the office. I suggested that McNamara play at 7:00 before others arrived.

So in 1962, we started that routine every Tuesday and every Thursday morning, and we still have that same schedule to this day, though we do not stick to it as rigorously as we did in the early years. Before long the secretary had improved his game so that he no longer felt self-conscious; and by this time other people were also playing at the 7:00 A.M. hour. The secretary had in fact started a trend. In the early years he arrived in his chauffeur-driven limousine. In the later years he drove himself in a small Ford.

One thing about Bob McNamara that stood out was his punctuality. He would show up for a lesson or game at exactly two minutes before the scheduled time, and he would depart immediately after the game was over. On the court it was all tennis and no nonsense and usually very little small talk. This has been the routine for over forty years, except for one occasion when he was about fifteen minutes late. I suspected that disaster must have struck. It turned out that his watch had stopped.

On another occasion, he failed to show up altogether. Later that day he sent his driver over to personally apologize, who explained that McNamara's absence was caused by something going on at "The Bay of Pigs."

After almost forty years of playing tennis with Robert McNamara, I still feel like I do not truly know him. I respect the man, and know that he is a truly decent, caring person. His tenure at the World Bank was exemplary. But I cannot support his actions during the Vietnam War. Even his own children, I understand, were not in total agreement with his Vietnam policies. More than anything else, I think he saw himself as a team player and adopted a "my country right or wrong" philosophy. However, we never discussed politics on the court.

Another couple who played regularly were Cyrus and Grace Vance. They first came to Washington in the

1960s and joined the club then. Cy had a high position in the Kennedy administration but had the brains and the courage to get out when government policies conflicted with his own principles. Cy and Gay, as they were known, and their children spent a fair amount of time on the tennis courts at St. Albans during the sixties. They had an old topless Jeep that would often fail to start and they would have to push the vehicle to get it running down the hill and then jump start it as they passed the tennis courts. The Vances left Washington and then came back during the Carter years when Cy took over as secretary of state. Gay contacted me before they arrived to tell me how much they looked forward to returning and that one of the main attractions of coming back to Washington was to be able to play at St. Albans. I could not help asking her at the end of the conversation if she had ever found a new battery for the old Jeep. This was an unspoiled family of decent people who believed in service and practiced it.

I remember one morning while sitting at my desk in the tennis office at 6:30 A.M., seeing a man with a broom walking past the shop toward the courts. He was an African American, and I assumed it was James Grayson, my trusted co-worker, who was known by all as simply "Grayson." I looked again and discovered that it was Andy Young, at that time probably congressman from Georgia, who had arrived early and was helping Grayson by sweeping the lines.

Robert Manning, who handled press releases for the State Department and later went on to become editor of the *Atlantic Monthly* was another pupil of mine. He had a set time each week for his lesson, but because of a great many emergencies and the traveling he had to do he often had to cancel his lessons. For a number of weeks he had missed his appointment. Finally he was able to make a date. That day, for some reason, I had to stop at the little shop between lessons and heard the phone ring. The caller asked for Manning. Knowing that his work kept him from playing tennis, I wanted to give him as much opportunity as possible to stay on the court. "Is it important?" I asked the caller. The answer was, "Yes. I am assistant to the president of the United States and the president wants to speak to Bob immediately. He'd better get to the phone!" Bob later returned with a sheepish look on his face saying that President Kennedy quipped, "So that's where you guys spend all of your time!"

Sandra O'Connor, though she is not a member of the club, has always played a lot of doubles there. One day she was late for a doubles game because the telephone repairman was at her house and she couldn't leave until he finished his work. "My partners are going to kill me!" she exclaimed. "Would you pass this information on to them?" After this message, a half hour passed and a second message similar to the first came through. Needless to say, she missed the game.

I played social doubles with Sandra on a couple of occasions. Usually when playing social doubles, I would slow down to one-half to three-quarters speed to try to keep the game competitive for our opponents. My partners who were good players would usually do the same. Not so for Justice Sandra Day O'Connor, who played with a take-no-prisoners fierceness that left our opponents in the dust. She was a true competitor who enjoyed winning by as wide a margin as possible.

OTHER CELEBRITIES

Generally speaking, people in Washington are not all that impressed with political celebrities. There are just too many of them. Try to have a tennis celebrity match with politicians and it is likely to be a failure unless attended by lobbyists or businessmen, who pay for the benefit of knowing a person with influence.

However, the people who are not impressed with political celebrities and who would not walk across the street to see a senator or a cabinet officer are often smitten by entertainment celebrities. I remember once being at one of the late Phil Stern's birthday parties. Phil was an important part of Washington as heir to the fortune of Sears Roebuck. He was quite active in arts and politics. In fact, his book on the inequities of the tax system at the time was often quoted in the media. Many celebrated figures attended this party—writers, artists, statesmen, and famous lawyers, as well as non-celebrity friends of Phil. I arrived and headed for the bar. Before reaching the watering hole, however, I was met by at least three different friends who informed me that Charlie Rose had Bill Cosby play tennis with him that afternoon at St. Albans. These sophisticated Washingtonians were awed by Cosby. Another time, even someone as prominent and well-traveled as Jack Valenti, a regular tennis player at St. Albans, who was exposed to the world's most important people when he was working for President Lyndon Johnson, seemed to savor the situation when he paraded entertainer Pat Boone in front of the regular tennis players at St. Albans. The same is true for the younger generation. St. Albans students are accustomed to seeing the vice president, famous TV personalities, and politicians all the time. Yet when Elizabeth Taylor, who at the time was married to John Warner, the senator from Virginia, stopped by St. Albans when the senator's son John was a student there, the school came to a complete standstill.

The famous personalities were not always political and not always local. "Do you remember Bernard Destremau?" The question came from Jim Lowenstein, a former ambassador to Luxemburg and then a high-ranking member of the State Department. "He is here in Washington and wants to play some tennis." Since Destremau was in my age bracket, I thought we could probably work something out. "By the way," Jim echoed, "he likes to be referred to by his formal title 'Mr. Foreign Minister.'" I then had to remind Jim that at the tennis club no one except Ben Cohen, Franklin Roosevelt's well-known advisor, was referred to as "Mr." anything and that was only because of his octogenarian status. Furthermore, Destremau's official position was actually French *deputy* foreign minister, not foreign minister.

The next afternoon Bernard Destremau arrived at the courts accompanied by an entourage. A chauffeur brought him and someone else carried his rackets. I mentioned that I thought he played his best tennis just before the war. He then gave me his record of winning the French doubles in 1938 and reaching the semifinals in the United States doubles championship at Forest Hills, plus many years of representing France in Davis Cup matches. "How about you?" he queried. "Oh," I replied, "I just hack around in some of the senior tournaments."

After we warmed up a while, I won the first set 6–0, and Destremau started swearing in French. We started a second set, and I did everything possible not to disgrace this rather pretentious person. I played balls that were out and called others in. I even finagled the score as much as I could, the result of which was that we were able to quit at 4–all. That night, Lowenstein, who could not wait to find out the results, called me at home. I replied, "I hope I did not set back diplomatic relations," and described the tennis match. The next day when I was on the court I noticed a French automobile pull up and saw someone go into the tennis shop with a package. When I finished playing I asked Val Lubbers, my righthand administrator, "Who is your admirer?" "Oh," she said, "it's not for me. It's for you," and handed over a bottle of champagne sent by Destremau.

I was telling this story over lunch one day to John Scali, who had been a television journalist before embarking on a diplomatic career. John did me one better, describing a situation when he received a kilo of fresh caviar and a magnum of Dom Perignon after beating the ambassador of Iran, who was son-in-law to the shah.

The club has also had its share of "spooks," a word that I use to describe CIA agents who sometimes pose as employees of the State Department or Department of Defense, even though most of them, if they ever entered the State Department or the Pentagon, could not find their way out. In any event, I noticed that several of these spooks seemed to have marriage difficulties and even thought about writing an article, entitled "Why CIA Agents Make Poor Husbands." My supposition was that those in the covert operation field got so much practice in the art of deception that they started to think in such terms even when they didn't need to use false tactics. There certainly have been members of the club who were exceptions to the rule, but I believe my theory has some validity.

PRESIDENTIAL CANDIDATES

It is not that unusual at the St. Albans Club for a particular tennis player to announce his candidacy for president. When this happens, of course, he is given security by the Secret Service. This means that a guard always accompanies the candidate to the tennis courts. Over the years, St. Albans has been overrun with security detail both for presidential candidates as well as cabinet members who also have their own entourage of cleancut, well-dressed Secret Service agents.

Given the high profile of presidential candidates, press coverage and exposure have always been important issues at the club. I was playing with Katherine Graham, the publisher of *The Washington Post,* when Eugene McCarthy, a presidential candidate at the time, walked behind our court on the way to another court. I found Gene McCarthy to be extremely bright, in fact well ahead of most of the other politicians. When we played together we spent a lot of time at the net telling stories and joking about some of the characters in politics. His tenure in the Senate was punctuated by a lot of strife during the Vietnam War, and he became a mythic figure to his many devoted followers as he pursued his ultimately unsuccessful run for the presidency.

As McCarthy crossed behind our court, he snidely remarked that he hoped that *The Washington Post* didn't object to his playing tennis, apparently upset over some recent criticism he had received from the paper. When she realized who he was, Katherine Graham muttered something under her breath, and told me later that she felt the *Post* had been very fair to McCarthy.

Kay Graham went on, of course, to become the best selling author of her memoirs, and her literary style and openness was a surprise to many people because she had been such a private person and had tried to avoid publicity. In fact, when obnoxious reporters wanted stories on what celebrities were doing at St. Albans, I would usually mention something about the Grahams, knowing full well that a story about the publisher of the *Post* was absolutely taboo for them to write about. I can remember Katherine Graham driving by the club and telling me that her husband Phil was doing so well at Chestnut Lodge, where he was under treatment for an emotional disorder, that she wanted to hit some tennis balls with him and asked me if I could lend her a spare racket. This turned out to be the tragic day that he killed himself.

Kay Graham was succeeded as the publisher of the *Post* by her son Donald, a job he handled with success. After college Don went to Vietnam to learn what was happening there, and then decided to become a D.C. policeman for several years, a rather unusual job for a Harvard graduate and heir to a newspaper dynasty. On the tennis court, he has always been an excellent player, who tends to be overly generous to his opponents. His sister and two brothers were also pupils of mine when they were young.

On one occasion my wife, Peggy, and I were invited to a small dinner party at Gene McCarthy's apartment, along with the poet in residence at the Library of Congress. McCarthy read a poem that he had quoted to me before, to the effect of "the vice president should be a tennis pro because he makes you look much better than you are." Then he said, "Allie, you ought to be the vice president." It is true that as a tennis pro I try to make my pupils look as good as possible and often feed the ball to their advantage. In games this is known as "customer tennis." McCarthy used to say that when I played with Robert McNamara, I played to his strength so much that after hitting strong forehands following his 7:00 A.M. lesson McNamara would go back to the Pentagon and escalate the war.

I also taught presidential aspirant George McGovern, who was one of the most decent individuals that I have ever had the pleasure of meeting. We just played for exercise and enjoyment. I don't know if he ever learned how to keep score. When he was nominated at the Democratic Convention, he left at some godforsaken early hour and was so nervous and excited that I doubt he could even sleep. At 9:00 A.M. on Saturday morning following the nomination, I got an emergency call at home, "Allie, this is George McGovern." "Congratulations, George," I remarked. He continued, "I know you don't work on weekends, but would you mind playing some tennis with me?" Because he was being followed closely by the press and wanted to shake them, we could not play at St. Albans. I recommended that we play at one of my friend's homes where there was a private court. McGovern immediately thought of Hickory Hill, the home of Ethel Kennedy, which also had a private court and where McGovern had enjoyed playing from time to time. Since Ethel was out of town and George and Liz Stevens were housesitting, this seemed the better choice. So that morning McGovern and I went out to Hickory Hill to play tennis. He was very excited about the upcoming campaign.

As the campaign progressed, the candidate and his staff went to the Black Hills of South Dakota and I went along with them. We stayed in rustic cabins on the lake. I had free run of the camp. George gave me the telephone number at his cabin so that we could arrange our tennis dates. Finally we located a court, in fact, the only court in Custer County, situated just behind the community center of a church. Because the court did not have side fences or net posts, we had to tie the net, which we found in the garage, to a tree. The Secret Service limousine would drive us the eight miles or so to the tennis court, which gave us a chance to talk about the campaign. I attended a strategy session and found it fascinating. Later I joined the staff for dinner, where some of them ate buffalo steak. At that time the group expressed great optimism. Charles Guggenheim, prize-winning documentary film maker, was also there, and we started a friendship that lasted for many years, until his recent death. Representative Walter Fauntroy from the District of Columbia spent the evening entertaining us with his songs.

The next morning there was supposed to be a press conference. For some reason the appointed time came and went, and a number of us were waiting outside the building to be let in. I was talking to Grace Bassett, who covered politics for one of the syndicated news agencies, and to Sander Vanocur, who was working for one of the television networks. Senator Tom Eagleton had been chosen as McGovern's running mate, and the Eagletons had been campaigning in Hawaii. Eventually the group arrived and Barbara Eagleton stopped to say hello to me, and we chatted as we entered the building. Something in the air just did not seem right.

The conference started with Tom Eagleton responding to a reporter's question about his depression and having received psychiatric help. How well I remember the beads of sweat rolling down his face as he answered questions put to him about his mental health. The campaign, of course, never recovered from this event.

Our tennis date was postponed until a little later in the day while the candidates struggled with the problem presented by the revelations about Eagleton. Finally, when McGovern and I headed out for the court, I figured I would get the lowdown on the situation. We had not gone very far, however, when someone George recognized flagged us down and asked to come along with us. It turned out to be a reporter so I did not get a chance to discuss the issue. Moments later, a *Washington Post* reporter spotted me and figured out what McGovern was doing, ending the privacy of our tennis game as the TV news crews managed to capture us hitting balls.

Eventually Eagleton dropped out and was replaced by Sargent Shriver. Sarge was not a bad tennis player. I remember one year I applied to play at the Wimbledon Veterans Doubles Tournament but was not accepted. Shriver had made it, however, leaving me to believe that even though he was a pretty good tennis player, the selection had more to do with social factors than with merit. Though Sarge never became vice president, in my opinion he did a great job as an ambassador and as head of the Peace Corps.

Toward the end of the McGovern campaign, I received a call from his office. At that point, he was spending more time at his house on the Eastern Shore of the Chesapeake Bay and suggested that I come down for the day. It was a modest house, but there was a tennis court only a few steps away. Only a few people were there: Eleanor, his wife, two or three from his office, and Dick Veleriani, a television newsman from NBC who had also been a pupil of mine. We played social tennis, had some refreshments and tried to keep our spirits up. But it was quite evident the outlook at that point was pretty bleak and the chance of a victory slim. The election turned out to be a landslide defeat. I always admired George McGovern. So much of what he stood for has been borne out to be true, especially his views about Vietnam.

Another candidate for president who played at the club was Walter Mondale, or Fritz as he was better known to us. He and Joan lived in the Cathedral neighborhood called Cleveland Park in an old house whose interior they painted themselves. The house was only a few blocks from the tennis courts. Joan had her doubles group with Nancy Stevenson, Adlai Jr.'s wife; Barbara Eagleton; and future White House social secretary Gretchen Posten. It also included Mary Sasser, the lovely wife of Jim Sasser, senator from Tennessee and later ambassador to China.

Fritz took lessons early in the morning and enjoyed the exercise. He always had a good sense of humor. His wife Joan also seemed to enjoy her position as wife of the vice president. She was very active in social causes and in the arts, was chauffeured in a limousine, and had body guards for protection. A week after her husband left office I saw her in the neighborhood walking her dog. She was wearing jeans and was not recognized, just another one of the local residents.

The tennis club had a number of other candidates for president. In addition to Mondale, McGovern, and McCarthy, Lloyd Bentsen, Fritz Hollings, Larry Pressler, Gary Hart, George H. W. Bush, and Lamar Alexander all were regular tennis players at St. Albans.

Although Albert Gore, Jr., had attended St. Albans as a student, he did not play tennis. For a short period of time, his son was at the school. Occasionally one would see Gore on campus watching some of his son's athletic contests. The last time I saw Al Gore on the school grounds he was on his way to see a game on the athletic field just above the tennis courts, and in a semi-panic he ran up to me and asked, "Allie, do you have a men's room here?"

DIVORCES

One of the more sensitive membership issues at the St. Albans Tennis Club is what happens when a couple is divorced. Early in the club's history, Peggy Ives, a good friend and regular tennis player, sent in her tennis renewal, following her recent divorce. At the same time Steve Ives, her ex-husband, sent in a renewal with his new mate. This presented a serious problem because we had only a limited number of members and the divorce rate in Washington was and still is relatively high. Therefore, we had to come up with some kind of a policy related to divorce because quite often both husband and wife played tennis. If each took on a new partner, membership would soon double and this Malthusian expansion simply would not be supportable.

We set a rule that the club membership would be decided at the time of the divorce proceedings. If no decision was made, we would continue to honor the individuals as members just as before. But we would not automatically allow a divorced member to bring in a new spouse. Rather, the new spouse would go on the waiting list and be treated like any other person on the wait list. This was a small step, I thought, in the direction of not promoting sexism.

While this policy was generally well received by the members, some people were not happy when they found themselves with new partners or spouses who were good tennis players but could not immediately join the club. Art Buchwald, a regular member, considered the policy so amusing that he ended up writing one of his funnier columns about it.

Several divorcees never used the courts themselves but steadfastly paid their half of the dues so that their ex-husbands could not bring in their new wives. Of course, inevitably, some people tried to sneak in their new partners despite the rules. With "live-ins" this often turned out to be easier than with marriages. In any event, I told members that while I was not going to demand a marriage license inspection prior to playing tennis, if the new mate wanted to be a member, he or she would have to appear in the directory so that it would be public knowledge. I also suggested that they should seriously consider consulting a lawyer before taking any action. In fact when I explained the policy to a noted law professor, he held off putting his lady friend in the directory until after they were married. I have been told that the subject of membership in the St. Albans Club has been a point of major contention in more than one divorce settlement.

STAYING WITH THE CLUB

When St. Albans Tennis Club members leave town, they have the option of becoming inactive members. For a small annual fee, we will hold the membership open until they return. This has always worked well for diplomats who go on three-year tours of duty, as well as others who come and go out of Washington on a regular basis. A number of cabinet members who had previously been to Washington were able to keep their memberships open. Cyrus Vance and Warren Christopher are examples of ranking government officials who benefitted from holding their memberships open when they returned as cabinet members after being away from Washington for several years.

Allie with sister Sylvia, c. 1928.

Allie with brother Abe.

Allie, c. 1928.

Ritzenberg Tennis Duo Triumph

Battle for Public Parks Singles Title

"Ritzenberg has a chance to cop two crowns in the tourney in the match today at 3 o'clock at the Reservoir Courts. Yesterday he and his brother Hy defeated Harry March and Ray Stocklinski for the doubles honors."
(*Washington Star,* summer 1937)

Peggy and Allie on his return from the
Pacific in 1945.

llie, Chief Justice Earl Warren, and Pauline Betz Addie, at an exhibi-
on match at the Sheraton Park Hotel, c. 1957. *(credit: Robert Striar)*

llie, Jimmy Van Alen, Lew Hoad, and Jack Kramer just after Hoad
nd Kramer had tested out, in an exhibition match in Washington,
'an Alen's new scoring system, VASSS, which was subsequently
dopted by the United States Tennis Association in 1970.

Allie with Kay Graham before a lesson. *(credit: Diana Walker)*

Allie and Art Buchwald. *(credit: Joy Carter)*

Allie with Bob McNamara after an early morning lesson.
(credit: Diana Walker)

Sen. Strom Thurmond (R), Sen. Chuck Perry (R), and
Rep. Jimmy Symington (D) at a Republicans vs. Democrats match.
(credit: Joy Carter)

Just after his nomination at the Democratic Convention in 1972, George McGovern manages to play tennis without the press watching, at the home of Ethel Kennedy. *(credit: Fred Ritzenberg)*

Allie and Peggy at his eightiethth birthday party.

Allie with Bobby Riggs, recipient of a Washington Tennis and Education Foundation Annual Award.

Allie with granddaughter Leah Winn-Ritzenberg, c. 1988. *(credit: Jane Gwaltney)*

Allie and Nate in Florida.

A different case was that of Michael Blumenthal, secretary of the Treasury under President Carter, who kept his inactive status open for many years before dropping it when it finally became apparent that he would not be returning to Washington. Donna Shalala knew that she would return to Washington, and so did I. She left Washington after working with the Carter administration when she worked for the Department of Housing and Urban Development (HUD), taking on the presidency of Hunter College in New York and later the University of Wisconsin. But she still sent her annual $35 membership fee. It was no surprise to receive a letter from Donna that she was coming back to fill the Health and Human Services cabinet post under President Clinton. She was a pretty good tennis player and had a standing lesson scheduled for one day each week.

ST. ALBANS SCHOOL

The other part of my job at St. Albans was to direct the tennis program for the school and to coach the tennis team. I enjoyed this job as well. My philosophy was to encourage as many young people in the school as possible to learn to love the game of tennis so that in the years to come they would be able to enjoy the spirit, sportsmanship, and the physical and emotional benefits derived from the game.

The classes were filled with fifty students. The varsity and junior varsity were all "homegrown" kids who tended to be more interested in competition and in winning. St. Albans did not provide tennis scholarships. In competition, the St. Albans team did well, but we did not usually match up to schools that recruited nationally ranked players.

We did, however, produce some good tennis players. Perhaps the best was Bo Jones, who became the top junior player in the area and later went on to play at Harvard, where he was awarded a Rhodes Scholarship. Bo is currently publisher of *The Washington Post.* Another great player was Randy Kennedy, also a Rhodes Scholar and now a professor at Harvard Law School and author of several books.

COACHING

As tennis coach at St. Albans, while I believed that winning was important, winning was never the primary goal. The problem with so many athletic programs today is that they focus almost exclusively on winning. I have heard many stories of abuse by coaches and parents who are pushing kids for the sake of their own glorification, not with the interests of the children in mind. This seems to be especially true of coaches and parents who never were great athletes themselves. By driving their pupils with long hours of repetition and inhumane work, they attempt to play the role of the first sergeant who drills and drills to make up for his own lack of knowledge. Many of these parents hope to enhance their own self-esteem through their children's success. This has never been my approach. Rather, I have tried to stress participation and learning a sport that can stay with an individual for the rest of his or her life.

The vicarious living of parents and the excessive ego of many coaches should be recognized for what they are and measures should be put in place to prevent the abuse of young people. Parents, however, seem to be demanding greater and greater emphasis on their children's varsity sports, often intimidating school administrators. Furthermore, the changes demanded by parents often affect only about 10 percent of the students at a school. The improvements are available only for the varsity players, and the new facilities really are not of much value to nonathletes. Too many times kids who want to play for recreation in order to bolster physical and emotional well-being are passed over in favor of the young people who thrive on competition. Unfortunately, it seems to be the parents of the children who are the noisiest and often the most obnoxious who tend to get the ear of school administrators.

In the case of tennis, the real emphasis needs to be long-term enjoyment of the game. As a practical matter, only a small percentage of tennis players play in tournaments, leagues, or ladders, or are good enough to play on a highly competitive level. Most simply want to enjoy the game, get exercise, and have fun with friends. This has been the essence of my philosophy in tennis and is what I have tried to instill both in young people and adults.

On one occasion, I was coaching a student whose father was well known both nationally and internationally. Just as the team was ready to leave for the other school, I could not find the young man. One of the team players located him in the library and we quickly put him in the waiting vehicle. It was a hot day and he never took his jacket off during the match. On the court, his hitting seemed erratic. The youngster was one of the nicest and most gentle kids that I had known, but more than likely he was intimidated by the stature of his father. It became apparent to me that on this particular day the reason the young man was playing so poorly was he had been drinking. I could not go to the opposing coach and say that my player was not capable of playing because he was not sober. Because of the youngster's poor performance, he appeared to be playing in a higher slot than he should have been in, a situation that prompted the opposing coach to accuse me of stacking the lineup. This was the only time in my career that I was ever accused of cheating. It was painful watching the player get humiliated by a much weaker player, and a relief when the match was finally over.

Following the match, we called in the student's parents and other teachers. We discussed the problem, and the young man's performance and behavior subsequently improved.

TENNIS AT THE WHITE HOUSE

Beginning during my tenure at the Sheraton and lasting into the St. Albans years, I had the honor of playing tennis at the White House. After my initial meeting with Jackie Kennedy when we found ourselves on all fours chasing her errant terrier, we started a routine of tennis lessons on the White House courts. Through these lessons, I got to know her and members of the Kennedy extended family. The lessons were fun and the relationship that I developed with Jackie was relaxed and informal.

I remember at one point during a lesson Jackie mentioning that the president should be getting more exercise and opining that he should be hitting some tennis balls as well. I told her that I had an old ball-throwing machine, which no longer was being used, and that I would be happy to send it down to the White House court for him to use, but it would need an electrical outlet. A gardener's shack sat next to the tennis court. We concluded there must be an electrical outlet in it. The door was locked so we found an unlocked window and the two of us crawled through the window into the dusty building, where we were able to find an outlet.

I sent the ball machine to the White House, though I do not know if it was ever used.

The White House court was actually very pleasant. A large magnolia tree standing next to the court was large enough so that the players were completely hidden from the public and were able to enjoy full privacy. The extensive landscaping around the court also helped, and I noticed some years later when I returned to the court in 1997 that the little shack that I had entered with Jackie Kennedy had been completely renovated and was being used as a changing room.

During one lesson that took place before an important state dinner, Jackie misjudged a ball, which caught her in the eye. It didn't do any damage, but we feared that it would result in a black eye for the evening occasion. Fortunately, it did not turn out to be noticeable. She looked fine for the evening.

During my lessons with Jackie, the president and Vice President Lyndon Johnson often strolled through the gardens and would stop at the court from time to time. One day when Jack Kennedy was walking alone on the grounds, he stopped to hit some tennis balls. He was dressed in a suit but removed his jacket and we played. It was obvious, however, that his back was bothering him and that he was in great pain.

The real tennis player in the Kennedy extended family was Ethel, who was a ferocious competitor and a very strong player. Bobby Kennedy was also pretty good, but he was not into tennis as much as his wife. One of the activities I enjoyed the most was the annual pet day at Hickory Hill, Ethel and Bobby's estate, when children from all over Washington would bring their pets. Ted Kennedy also was a member of the club for a number of years, but he never used the courts much.

Art Buchwald used to play a lot with the Kennedys. When he approached me about lessons and I suggested an eight o'clock time slot, he exclaimed, "Eight o'clock? You have got to be kidding! My eyes aren't even open at eight A.M., and I don't even begin to function until after ten."

Most of the time that I was teaching tennis to Jackie it was a secret. The Kennedys preferred privacy and did not want to publicize the fact that Jackie was getting tennis lessons. However, on one occasion one of Washington's most aggressive reporters approached me to have lunch at which time she asked me point blank, "Are you teaching Jackie Kennedy tennis at the White House?" I responded that I did not discuss any of my pupils. At the same time, a woman in Michigan announced that she was being flown to Washington to give tennis lessons to the First Lady, an assertion that was vigorously denied by the White House. So they decided to act and broke the story that indeed Jackie was receiving lessons and that I was the coach. The lessons went on for two years and were one of my most enjoyable experiences during that period in my life.

Tennis history at the White House actually goes back some time. The court in Theodore Roosevelt's time was at a different location, situated next to the house. While Teddy Roosevelt himself was not a good player, he did have what was known as the "tennis cabinet."

The son of Warren Harding supposedly died from an infection that he got from the dye on his socks while playing tennis on the White House court. When the Kennedy administration came in, the players on the president's staff were not satisfied with the maintenance done by the Parks Department, so they personally contributed to the resurfacing of the courts, an action that unfortunately failed to produce very high-quality playing surfaces. President Johnson once said that he did not even know there were tennis courts at the White House, a statement which if true was inaccurate, since I had seen him several times while giving lessons to Jackie Kennedy. For whatever reason, I think he was trying to give the impression that tennis did not mean anything to him.

While the courts remained in fairly poor condition through the Kennedy and Johnson years, when Nixon arrived he had a friend, Donald Kendall, who managed to get Pepsi Cola into Russia and who picked up the bill for completely redoing the courts. It was a pretty good job, which I was able to inspect personally when I was invited to watch the match between the White House staff and the White House correspondents. Joe Blatchford, who was then director of the Peace Corps, played for the White House staff, and his popularity had grown after the well publicized event when his doubles partner Vice President Spiro Agnew hit him on the head with a serve. Thereafter Joe always wore a helmet when playing with Agnew.

President Jimmy Carter was not a good tennis player but had a staff that utilized the courts so frequently that a system with time limitations had to be established.

George H. W. Bush took great advantage of the courts. His parents, Senator and Mrs. Bush, had played at my courts at the Sheraton Park Hotel; and the president himself, while a member of Congress, often played at St. Albans with his wife, Barbara. His sons, Neil and Marvin, were excellent players and used the courts frequently, though neither George W. nor Jeb did. Marvin invited me to play at the White House when his father was president, but we were never able to get around to it. I take some pride, however, in the fact that I have taught or played tennis with three generations of the Bush family.

When the Clinton administration came to Washington after the 1992 election, St. Albans Tennis Club was home court to a number of cabinet members, including Warren Christopher, Donna Shalala, Ron Brown, Lloyd Bentsen, Les Aspin, Madeleine Albright and Larry Summers. Donna and Larry were probably the most avid players and used the courts several times a week. When Donna started taking lessons during her stint at HUD in the Carter administration, she had a weak forehand and had a long way to go as a player. When she departed Washington at the end of the Clinton years, she was an accomplished player. Larry was a very strong all-around player and tough competitor. On more than one occasion I would look out on the courts during an early morning time slot to witness a majority of the Clinton cabinet hitting balls.

DISCRIMINATION

I consider myself extremely lucky to have had the opportunity to see a part of Washington that few people outside the political elite ever get to see. I grew up in rather modest circumstances and was a Jew teaching at a premier WASP institution. I often wonder how this happened, especially since over the years discrimination against Jews has persisted.

When I was growing up in Washington, discrimination and segregation were taken for granted by school children. Schools were racially separated, and recreational facilities were available for white and "colored," but not in equal numbers. Most clubs were totally restricted by race or religion, and many neighborhoods had covenants that barred the sale to "colored" or non-Christian people.

The discrimination I personally felt from time to time made me aware of others being discriminated against, and instilled in me a determination that was responsible in part for my competitive drive. Perhaps without experiencing that discrimination, the drive would not have been as strong.

Following World War II no great rush to integrate social organizations was apparent in American society. Many of the tennis clubs were still divided on the basis of religion. The wealthier Jewish residents of large cities started their own clubs because they were prohibited from joining the established country clubs in the area.

When I obtained an application to join the Edgemoor Tennis Club in Bethesda shortly following the war, one of the questions asked for was the name of my college fraternity. I completed the application; but instead of sending it in, I put it in my safe deposit box. Many years later when applying to the club, I sent in the old application along with the new one.

I was determined in my career to oppose discrimination of any kind. When I started working at the courts at the Sheraton, one of the first things I did was to stage an exhibition between Althea Gibson and Shirley Frye, the Wimbledon finalists. It was the first time in Washington that black and white women had competed against each other in public.

The tennis clubs were slow to keep up with the cultural changes. During my early tenure at St. Albans, a member of Kenwood Country Club brought in entry blanks for a junior tournament there. These blanks were for members of the St. Albans Tennis Club he said; but when a young black boy turned in his entry, the tournament was immediately canceled.

We participated in a junior boys league comprised of various local teams. One day in 1965, I received a call from the manager of the Congressional Country Club, one of Washington's more elite institutions, who announced that their club was very busy and asked if we could host the competition at St. Albans rather than on their courts, where the match had been previously scheduled. The reason for the request, I strongly believed, was that they learned the competition was going to involve a black member playing at their club, a situation that they presumably considered unacceptable. In my most accommodating manner, I told him that while we too were a very busy place, we were also a patient club and would wait for Congressional to find a more suitable time for the match. They then dropped out of the league.

After that occasion, the father of a top junior player called me and spent about forty-five minutes on the phone haranguing me for the irreparable harm I was supposedly doing to junior tennis by being "not accommodating" and that I was responsible for the league breaking up. I told him that a bigger issue was at stake. It just so happened that several weeks later his son was playing tennis in Richmond, Virginia, where black players were not allowed to participate. However, the youngster showed his courage and protested, at which time several players withdrew from the tournament. To his credit, the young man's father called me to say that I had been right all along about the league play and that he had changed his mind. This young man, Harold Solomon, went on to reach the finals of the French Open and to became a great credit to the game, and one of the finest players ever produced in Washington. The young black man, Henry Kennedy, who was supposed to play in the Congressional match, went on to play on the Princeton team and later graduated from Harvard Law School, becoming the youngest United States magistrate in the country, an excellent judge, and a highly ranked tennis competitor.

Carl Rowan, noted columnist and former ambassador, and his wife, Vivien, were both original members of the club, and regular players at St. Albans. Carl was a good tennis player but not quite up to the caliber of Vivien. As an African American, Viv had felt the sting of discrimination when she was not allowed to play on a club team competing against a team from one of the country clubs in Washington. The Rowans lived in a fashionable Washington neighborhood that was predominantly white. One story about Carl is that he was working on his garden at the front of his yard when he was approached by one of his neighbors who wanted to know if he could also do some work for her. In his most pronounced southern drawl, Carl told her with a straight face, "You see, I have a special arrangement with the woman who lives in this house. I do the work in the garden and she lets me sleep with her."

Unfortunately, racial segregation has continued in one form or another for too long. Although when I took the position at St. Albans the school was integrated, many of the people who sent their children to the school lived in neighborhoods with restrictive covenants forbidding people to sell their homes to Jews, blacks, or in some cases foreigners from Eastern European countries. Neighborhoods like Wesley Heights, Spring Valley, and Westmoreland Hills had such covenants. It was often hard to change the views of people who had grown up in that culture. Despite persistent bigotry, conditions have changed for the better—albeit slowly—and I feel that I personally have benefitted from a more open society and have been accepted by what is primarily a WASP culture.

The St. Albans Tennis Club provided for me my last and best job, which still continues as I write this memoir some forty years after starting the club in 1962. Over the years the club has changed as one presidential administration goes out and another comes in; but compared to what has occurred in the rest of society, it has changed very little. The rules I established on day one are still pretty much the same. Players still wear whites and still must sign in; and the informal, relaxed atmosphere is as low key as ever. While many of the names have changed, more astonishing is that many have not. Some of the original members, such as Bob McNamara, still play, and there are a number of players my age or older.* The club is living testimony to the fact that tennis is a sport that can last a lifetime.

*The original membership of the St. Albans Tennis Club, in 1962, is listed in the appendix.

Alabaster sculpture

Acquired in an antique shop on the outskirts of Melbourne, Australia after an International Federation of Tennis senior championship

A. MICHELOTTI

1915 25" x 8" x 10"

CHAPTER 4

Senior Tour

In 1968, the year that the United States was going through much turmoil with student unrest, riots, and assassinations, the sport of tennis changed dramatically. This was the beginning of open tennis. In both the United States and abroad prior to 1968, the antiquated pristine tennis code did not allow professionals to vie against amateurs. The word "amateur" comes from the Latin root *amar,* meaning "to love." The idea was that amateurs played for the love of the game while professionals played for money. The problem, of course, was that tennis professionals were generally people who had so much love for the game that they made it a full-time career. Nonetheless, until 1968, those who benefitted financially were not able to compete with those who supposedly played only for the love of the game, which meant in effect that professionals were excluded from most of the major tournaments, never mind that many of these tournaments paid expense money under the table to the top players.

Prior to 1968, however, the professionals were not very well organized and the major source of money for those who did choose to compete was the barnstorming tours, in which only a small number of the very top players performed. Otherwise most pros were teaching pros like myself who worked at country clubs, resorts, or schools.

That year the first open tennis competition for seniors started at Forest Hills in New York when a seniors doubles championship was inaugurated for players forty-five and over. The tournament was held for two years, and I played doubles with Bob Ryland one year and Clark Taylor the next, both excellent players. We lost those years to Vic Seixas and Jaroslov Drobny not long after their prime. Shortly after this event the rules were changed for international competition as well.

Prior to open tennis, I had played in only a handful of professional tournaments as there were few to play in. With the advent of open tennis, however, I was able to prove to myself that I could play with my contemporaries who had achieved high rankings in amateur tennis and perform on an equal level with them. Fortunately, over the years the age categories have increased, due primarily to Alphonso Smith, who managed to get a new division created every time he reached a new five-year milestone. Now, the men's senior tournaments extend all the way up to the nineties. Recently, the patriarch of the Hyatt Hotel chain sponsored a tournament and gave free lodging to all the ninety-year-old players, including their wives or girlfriends.

The United States players involved in senior tennis run the gamut from tennis bums to the elite of corporate America. Many are medical doctors, some of whom have had to give lifesaving treatment to collapsed players from time to time. A number of players are well-known professors of economics, law, or history. Others are retired military officers, and there are a number of successful business tycoons. Tennis teaching pros like myself actually make up a very small percentage of tournament players. Rarely is there any prize money, and when there is, it does not cover the cost associated with playing. Except for the small number of name players, the participants in the senior tour pay all of their own expenses. Prizes are simple, and as far as I am concerned, the simpler the better. If you win a United States national championship—and there are four each year, one each on grass, clay, hard courts, and indoor courts—you get a gold ball. This trophy, however, is highly coveted. A few tournaments like to attract name players and will offer hospitality incentives, giving the winners free hotel accommodations for the next year.

Some of the better players in the senior tennis circuit have included Bobby Riggs, Gardner Mulloy, and Tom Brown—all Wimbledon winners. But the bulk of the players are those who never were among the great, though they generally play quite well and are in top physical shape. In fact, many of the well-known players of the past are so far out of condition that they would not be able to compete on the senior tour. Even Richard "Pancho" Gonzalez tried the senior tournaments for a while and then switched from singles to only playing doubles.

Some players, of course, are not very good and often never win a match, but they love it anyway and do not seem to mind defeat. Others, however, are ragingly competitive and will go all out for every point. Because most matches do not have umpires, the honor system prevails. I have seen some players who were the epitome of honesty until they became top players, at which point the pressure to win transformed some of these formerly lovely people into very close callers. In not so subtle terms, some have become cheaters.

The tour includes only a few mixed doubles seniors events. It takes a lot of energy to play both singles and doubles especially if one reaches the later rounds. To add a third competitive event, mixed doubles, often is more than most can handle. For that reason, I generally avoid the mixed doubles events. The matches get progressively more difficult as you proceed up the ladder; and when exhaustion sets in, injuries often occur.

The senior tour has been an extraordinary opportunity for me. It has taken me to every continent on the planet, and I have been able both to play tennis and to see many sights of the world. I have won local, sectional, national, continental, and even world championships. In fact, I am the winner of what now will become the last Soviet championship, which took place shortly before the dissolution of the Soviet Union. In that event, we practiced on the indoor courts of the KGB, the Soviet Intelligence Agency.

Being on the senior tour has given me a chance to prove myself. At times I am reminded of the scenario about the dancer who gave up a career to care for her family and missed the opportunity to be in the big time. Because I became a teaching pro early, I had to give up amateur competition and never had a chance to make it big. So when the opportunity presented itself following the 1968 change in tennis rules, followed closely by the creation of a senior tour, I decided that I would throw my hat in the ring and play against some of the big names in amateur tennis. I would show them that I was as good as they were and that I would have fared every bit as well as they did in amateur tennis. Over the years, I have satisfied myself that had I competed in amateur tennis I probably would have been a highly ranked international player.

I have played a number of memorable matches. My most remarkable early-round match occurred at a tournament in Porto Caras, Greece. The opponent was not what I would call a bad player. In fact, his style was pretty good, but he was inconsistent. I won the first three games without losing a point. The situation was rather amusing, and I continued at the same pace and won the entire set without giving up a single point. After the set it dawned on me that I might be able to go through the whole match without losing a point. It became a challenge to see just how far I could go. At 4–love in the second set, I still had not lost a single point. Realizing that this near-impossible feat might be within my grasp, nervousness started to set in. I was afraid that I would tighten up and start making errors. It is in times like this that the inevitable double fault happens. I took a deep breath and persevered. Though tense, I won the next two sets 6–0, 6–0, and did in fact go through the whole match without giving up a single point.

In the finals of the Dutch professional championship, I was playing doubles with Mohamed Ali Mobarek. He was left-handed and I was right-handed. At one point we both went for the same ball, and with a slashing forehand my racket caught the back of his hand. I looked around and saw that his hand was frozen. The match was immediately declared over, and he went for an x-ray, which fortunately showed that his hand was not broken. Mobarek had won the Egyptian championship and had then gone to Saudi Arabia to work for the royal family as a tennis pro. Some years later, when I introduced myself to his son, who was playing in the United States Open at Forest Hills, the first remark to come out of his mouth was a reminder about the incident involving his father's hand.

Despite the many benefits associated with the senior tour, the tour has some problems. The cultural differences can be great between the American way of doing things and the practices of other nations. The older United States players are more egalitarian than those who grew up in more elitist societies where only the upper classes play tennis. The Americans as a rule are more forgiving and believe in giving the other fellow a break. Along with the British, we have the sporting tradition of giving the benefit of the doubt to our opponent. At least that had been the tradition for a long time though it is now changing somewhat for the younger generation.

The Scandinavian countries generally follow that tradition. The differences are most pronounced in Germany, Austria, France, and Italy. Based on discussions with other players from these countries, I have concluded that their philosophy is that one must fend for oneself. Their view is that because nobody gives you a break, you need to take what you can get. Many of these players also seem to believe that because they are from the upper crust and grew up at the top of the class system, they are privileged and automatically entitled to get all the breaks.

As a result, many players from these countries in the older age brackets exhibit an overabundance of cheating on line calls where we have been taught in the United States that our opponent gets anything that is absolutely not out. In some other countries the opposite is true. Anything close goes to the caller.

I once participated in a tournament in a lovely coastal resort in France called La Boule. The matches were to start on Monday. I arrived on Sunday ready to play. Although I believed I was better than anyone in

Europe competing in the tournament, the organizers had failed to seed me. Along with two other foreign players, I was placed in a preliminary round, and we were bunched together so that we would eliminate each other, save for one player, by the end of the first round. I ran through my side of the draw with relative ease and ended up in the finals. Against all the rules the top-seeded player was automatically placed in the semifinals. Furthermore, he had dictated to the committee that he was going to make his initial appearance on Saturday.

Disturbed by the situation, I asked the committee to schedule his semifinal, which I thought would be an easy match for him, for Saturday morning so that we could play the finals in the afternoon. The committee responded that he might not want to play two matches on the same day. My response was that in that case they didn't have a final. I pulled out and instead set off for Paris, where the members of America's women's tennis team joined me for the Folies Bergere.

The senior players who are recognized are often catered to excessively. They usually announce when they will appear and when they expect to leave. On one occasion at the famous Badrut's Palace Hotel in St. Moritz, Switzerland, I won the singles by defeating Mirek Kizlink in the finals. We were also paired together as a doubles team, but because there were not enough entries in our age group, we were thrown in with the next lower age group, which resulted in much tougher competition. Laci Leganstein was the pro at the club and a very strong tennis player. His partner was also a good player.

Also competing was Budge Patty, an ex-Californian who had won Wimbledon and was living in Switzerland. He reluctantly came to the tournament because he did not like the high altitude or the clay courts. Nevertheless he was considered the strong favorite. His partner was a former Spanish Cup player who was well over the hill and not in the best of health. In fact, he died shortly after the match.

My partner and I were playing very well and were in the same half of the bracket as Budge Patty and his Spanish partner, Fernando Olozaga. Apparently it dawned on those running the tournament that Mirek and I were likely to beat the Spaniard and Budge, and if that happened, they would not make it into the finals. The next day we were looking at the draw sheet, and to our surprise, we found that we had been shifted over to the other bracket, an unprecedented move which meant that we would not have to play Budge and the Spaniard unless we got to the finals. The committee managed to manipulate the competition to get that team into the finals so that the hotel guests would not be disappointed. This never would have happened in America. It turned out that they were upset in the finals by the pair who beat us in the semifinals.

I have played in other tournaments in resort areas where it has been difficult to see the draw sheets, which are often kept under a table rather than being publicly displayed. Upon more than one occasion, I have had to wait hours for a scheduled match while the local hero was put on early and given what I believe are undue privileges. When I have vehemently complained, I have sometimes been labeled "an ugly American."

One year I won the Asian senior championship in Jakarta in my age bracket and also won the doubles with my partner, Mahindar Singh. He was an Indian descended from a long line of rajas, who was disinherited after converting to Christianity following his Oxford education. He was a very likeable, sweet guy, and we enjoyed playing doubles together. A few years later, he was the host of the Indian seniors event held in his hometown, Chandigar, the capital of Punjab. The town, designed by the famous French architect Le Corbusier, was interesting but not typical of India. Naturally I asked Mahindar if he would be able to play doubles with me. He hemmed and hawed and finally said that he would like for me to play doubles with S. S. Ray, who happened to be the governor of the state. When he said Ray was a "very keen" player, I knew that what he really meant was that Ray was not very good and Mahindar wanted me to be paired with him to give him the best opportunity to win. This turned out to be a correct assessment. We played a practice session at the governor's mansion on his private, highly manicured grass courts with turbaned, uniformed servants waiting on us and the others watching us play. It seemed as if we were in a Hollywood movie.

When the tournament started, we had to drop down one age bracket for the doubles, making the competition much tougher. Ray actually played pretty well, and we won our way to the semifinals when Ray's mother-in-law suddenly died and he had to rush off to London, unable to complete the tournament. I doubt that we would have been able to win, but we did remarkably well. Ray went on to become the ambassador to the United States; and I saw him on several occasions, including a Halloween party held at our house just a week after he arrived in the United States

I went on to win the singles championship in that tournament. The next year I went back to Asia to defend my title. This time the tournament was staged in Pattaya, a resort town in Thailand. I had hoped I would be able to play doubles with Mahindar again, but when I got to the tournament, I was informed that they wanted me to play with a retired general, who had been the top military man in the country and had been instrumental in keeping order—another one of those "keen" players. We survived until the finals, and in that game I virtually killed myself but to no avail. Mahindar chuckled and understood very well what was going on.

A top player can generally choose another in a high category as a partner, but in political situations he usually submits to playing with an inferior player if it might be to some political or social advantage for the home country or those running the tournament. One thing this setup accomplishes is to give others a fair chance rather than having a lopsided outcome. This does not only happen abroad. In several charity events in the United States I have been partnered with less experienced players. One of those was Ron Ziegler, who at the time was press secretary for President Nixon. Even though he was not an experienced player, I enjoyed playing with him and also enjoyed playing with his wife, who was paired with me in mixed doubles.

On one occasion Peg and I were in Poland for a senior tournament, which took place at the Baltic port of Sopot, a town located next to Gdansk and Gdinia. After I won the finals in that tournament, Peg and I wanted to do some sightseeing in what was formerly Danzig. It was midafternoon and thousands of people were walking toward the train station. We had heard a certain amount of grumbling at the stores but could not figure out why so many people were charging toward the train station.

When we were leaving that night, members of our tennis club insisted that they accompany us to the railroad station, but we told them that was not necessary. We were anxious to get to France where we could get some decent food, which was lacking in that communist country. We arrived in France to see headline banners about Poland. The people we had seen rushing the train station were the shipyard workers starting the Solidarity Movement. We did not understand it at the time, but the Poles were defying the Russians, and the consequences of the events that day would later be seen as a major historical turning point in the Cold War.

BOBBY RIGGS

One of the great tennis players of the era was Bobby Riggs, and most of my encounters with Bobby came during the years he played seniors tennis. He was undoubtedly one of the all time hustlers of the game and was quite proud of it. The term "con man" to describe Bobby may be a little strong, but it is close to being accurate. To his credit, he was a student of probability, and he understood the odds of everything he did, including every tennis shot. As a probability expert, he never hit the ball any harder than he had to in order to win a point. This did not make him a flashy player, only a winner.

Bobby also gambled on practically everything. We were at a tournament together in Puerto Rico where he placed a substantial bet with a much younger player. The bet was that the opponent could place four chairs anywhere on Bobby's side of the court and if a ball hit a chair, the other person won the point. Riggs had to chase around moving the chairs just before the younger player hit the ball. Bobby managed to win the bet.

Playing at Wimbledon in 1939, Bobby knew what he was doing and earned a good day's pay doing it.

Somehow he had accumulated enough money to place wagers on himself. Never known as a big serve-and-volley player, he was not expected to win an event on grass, so the odds against him were quite high. His doubles partner was Elwood Cook, who in singles had been ranked number seven in the United States but was not among the great players. Again, the odds were quite unfavorable for Riggs to win the doubles. Finally, he was quoted the odds on mixed doubles with partner Alice Marble, who went on to win the singles with few losses during the tournament.

The only catch was that in the warm-up tournament preceding Wimbledon at Queen's Club, Bobby and Alice had suffered an early-round humiliating defeat. As a result, the odds on the mixed doubles for the Riggs-Marble team soared as well. This manipulation enabled Bobby to parlay his bets on winning all three events, which would be an extraordinary achievement. He beat Cook in the singles finals. He and Elwood won the doubles. Alice Marble and Bobby dominated the mixed doubles matches. Bobby Riggs walked away with a lot of money.

During World War II Bobby had been a recruit at the Great Lakes Naval Station. The new recruits were confined to barracks for several weeks. Bobby, however, was determined not to stay on the base and announced to his friends that he was going to get a pass. "Want to bet?" was the typical response. To which he responded, "Yes," and immediately started taking bets.

At that time Vice President Henry Wallace, an ardent tennis player, was in Chicago and requested that Riggs play him in a game. The commanding officer was not about to see the vice president disappointed. Again, Bobby was able to beat the odds and to cash in on his bets.

In 1988, Riggs was playing tennis in the age-seventy category and still playing at a very high level. By that time he had made the decision to limit his play to doubles in order to conserve his energy. His partner was Ed Doane, an exceptionally talented doubles player. That year they were playing pretty well.

Although I had played against Riggs a few times in previous seniors events—and he usually beat me in close matches—that year, matched with four different doubles partners, I faced Riggs and Doane in the finals of every one of the four major championships in seniors competition. Two of the tournaments were held in the West while the other two were held in the East. In the first tournament, the hard court championship at Santa Barbara, Bobby and Doane beat my partner and me in a very close match.

In the indoor championships, I played with Dan Walker and they beat us again, though some confusion remains about what exactly happened in that game. Some years later at a tournament in Los Angeles I saw Ed and we reminisced about the four matches that year. Although we can't always remember our children's birthdays or to bring home a loaf of bread, tennis players when challenged often can remember every point in a match. I mentioned that my partner missed an easy shot at the net on one of two match points. "No," Doane said, "you had *three* match points before you lost."

At the third national event that year, we played the grass court championship in Cedarhurst, Long Island. This time I had another partner and, again, we lost a three-set match.

The last match of the year was at the Army-Navy Country Club across the river in Arlington, Virginia. The tournament meant a great deal to Riggs, who wanted a clean sweep of the four national titles. This was as important to him, he said, as winning Wimbledon. This time I was partnered with George Young of northern California. Our opponents were leading in the final set when a light rain developed, and the committee stopped play. Riggs wanted to push ahead and finish and was quite vocal in his demands. We were ordered back on the courts and things started to look up for us after we saved our match on two championship points. Bobby was insulting the umpire and growing more troublesome. My partner and I finally won the championship in another hard-fought and tense set. Bobby was livid and his woman friend did not wish to be with him. She found solace in a drink or two and avoided Bobby until the next day.

I saw Bobby use every form of gamesmanship over the years. One player was giving him a rough time on the court. When the player would get ready to serve,

Riggs—instead of directing the ball to the server—would hit one into the corner of the fence and the next ball into the opposite side. He kept doing this, driving his opponent mad, causing him to lose concentration and subsequently the match.

What most people remember about Riggs is the famous nationally televised match in September 1973 when Billy Jean King beat him in the "battle of the sexes." People have asked me how Billy Jean—who was a great player in her own right—was able to beat him and whether Riggs threw the match. Of course, I do not know, but I do know that Riggs was known to lose a match or two when losing would mean a rematch and a bigger purse. If that is what he was hoping for, this was one bet where he miscalculated the odds. The rematch was not to be.

When matches got close, you could confidently place your bet that Bobby would emerge victorious. He had an extraordinarily complex personality, a huge ego, and super self-confidence.

NATE

I am not the only Ritzenberg who has been a tennis professional. My brother, Nate, has played professional tennis all his adult life as well. It is one of those ironic twists in life that two brothers who were so close and shared the sport of tennis could pretty much lose touch with each other, but that is what happened. After high school he went his way and I went mine. Nate taught and coached tennis at the club level throughout the South, but mainly in Florida; and because he does not like to travel, he did not participate in many tournaments outside Florida. So our paths did not cross.

A few years ago in 2000, however, I played in the over-eighty United States clay court championships at the Army-Navy Country Club in Arlington, Virginia. By the luck of the draw, my opponent in the second round was my brother. I was eighty-two at the time and Nate was eighty-four. We had not met in competition since the 1930s, and I had neither seen him nor heard much from him since then. Also in the tournament was Powell "Boots" Taylor of Norfolk, Virginia, another old friend who in 1934 had won the Middle Atlantic eighteen and under junior championship. Nate was victorious in 1935 and I captured that championship in 1936.

Now, over sixty-odd years later, the three of us were playing in the same tournament after each had won national championships. Nate was my opponent, and Boots was my partner in doubles competition. Playing against Nate in the singles match, I doubt that I have ever concentrated as hard or played such flawless tennis in my whole career. Rain forced the match indoors, where the courts were much faster and more suited to my game, and I finally beat my brother. Nate has always been in fabulous physical shape and plays a very steady game. Certainly there was some sibling rivalry between us.

Nate was a teaching pro himself before retiring. His lifestyle, however, is the opposite of mine in almost every way except for his strong emphasis on health and tennis. He eats one meal a day composed of boiled vegetables, lives in a modest home, has never driven a car, probably does not own a suit or tie, and cares very little about material possessions. By following a natural lifestyle, he doesn't expect to experience illness, so the lifestyle has served him well.

He plays tennis in long white slacks and still uses only wooden rackets. In fact, in 1992 he won the national clay court championship in theseventy-five-and-over category using a wooden racket. In 2002 he got to the finals in the eighty-five-and-over category. He is thin as a rail and has a young person's body. He doesn't travel much because he doesn't fly and rarely eats out because the restaurants don't accommodate his taste in foods. However, he is one of the most self-satisfied persons I have ever met and seems completely happy in his own world. He has been married three times and has one daughter, whom I have not seen in over fifty years.

As this manuscript was undergoing its final edit, I received a letter from Nate's wife, Alma, telling me that he was dying. I called him, but he was too weak to talk about his condition. Within a few days, he died. It turned out that Nate had been ill for a while, but, as was his way, he didn't consult with a doctor and whatever it was, probably cancer, finally won out.

NEVER GIVING UP

One of my more memorable senior tournaments occurred in 1997 in Buenos Aires, Argentina. The week before I had won the championship in Brazil, and I was defending my title in Buenos Aires in the age-seventy-five-and-over bracket. In fact, I had dominated the tournament the previous two years. Playing in the finals, my left leg suddenly gave in. I had torn a ligament and was limping quite badly. My opponent, sensing what had happened, kept moving me about and the match turned around completely.

I was now down in the final set, unable to get around the court. Knowing that I lacked mobility, I decided to change tactics and hit the ball as hard as I could on every shot, taking significant risks. I hit a hot streak and couldn't miss, ending up winning the match and the championship.

Following that game, I still had the doubles to play. This time we were playing in a lower age group, making the championship much more challenging. My partner, Bob Howe, had picked up an intestinal infection and had just finished the finals in his age group. He was both sick and weak, making frequent trips to the bathroom. Given my condition and his, I suggested that we forget about the match, as another championship was really not all that important. Bob had also won his share of championships, including winning Wimbledon in mixed doubles. We agreed to have lunch and decide what to do.

Strangely enough, we felt that we should give it one last try and then default if our health was not up to playing. Our match went three sets, lasting for two and a half hours. We both were hurting with every shot, but we persevered and won.

The senior tour has been on the whole a very rewarding and fulfilling experience, though at times it has been frustrating and tiring. I am even a little surprised when I recall all the tournaments I have played in over the years and how far I got in many of them: I managed to win a number of world championships, as well as the European and Asian titles and the championships of the United States, Canada, Soviet Union, Czechoslovakia, Poland, Yugoslavia, Argentina, Switzerland, Monaco, Spain, Germany, India, Israel, and Brazil. I also have also been a finalist in major tournaments in Italy, Hungary, Austria, England, France, China, Greece, Australia, and Mexico. This year I was surprised and honored to learn that the International Tennis Federation had ranked me number one among players eighty-five and over. In addition to allowing me the opportunity to prove to myself and to others that I was capable of playing at a high level, the senior tour gave me a chance to see the world and to meet a lot of very interesting people with very diverse backgrounds.

Doulton Lambeth salt glazed stoneware bowl (two views)

MARSHALL & MARY ANN THOMPSON

1881 15" x 7"

CHAPTER 5

What Have They Done to My Game?

Over my lifetime I have seen vast changes in tennis, some good, some bad. Some of these changes have developed with the popularization of tennis, a trend that I have strongly supported and contributed to. Some of these changes, however, have caused me to say to myself from time to time, "What have they done to my game?"

THE EVOLUTION OF TENNIS

For a long time tennis had the reputation of being a snobbish game played at exclusive clubs, mainly restricted to white people from northern European backgrounds. To a certain extent this stereotype was true in the United States except for areas with good public facilities such as California and some major cities such as Washington, D.C. Indeed, were it not for the good public facilities in Washington I may never have taken up tennis myself.

One look at the college championship records reveals a lot about the history of tennis. Between 1883, when the first national intercollegiate men's singles championship was held and 1923, every winner of that event was enrolled in an Ivy League school, with two exceptions. In 1886, G. M. Brentley from Trinity College in Connecticut won, and in 1921, Philip Haer from Stanford won. Harvard players won sixteen times during this period, while Yale accounted for eight victories and Princeton for five.

With one or two exceptions, 1922 was the last time that an Ivy League student won the college championship in either singles or doubles. In the early 1920s change began to occur, as several California colleges, as well as Tulane, Rice, and the University of Texas won tournaments. Southern schools won the majority of tournaments in the 1940s; and in the late 1950s the era of domination by California schools began—UCLA, the University of Southern California, and Stanford.

Tennis became increasingly popular in metropolitan areas after the Depression, and while suffering a setback with the onset of World War II, the sport picked up again in popularity following the end of hostilities. America was becoming increasingly prosperous and people were beginning to have more leisure time to devote to recreational activities. Golf was the most popular and certainly the most high-profile sport during the Eisenhower years, with tennis taking a back seat.

After Eisenhower left the White House, however, an entirely new group of individuals arrived on the scene in Washington. These were young, dynamic, bright intellectuals who worked hard and played hard. They did not have time to spend hours on the golf course and had to get exercise in capsule form. This situation certainly contributed to the popularity of tennis in Washington, and perhaps in other urban centers as well.

At about the same time, Dr. Paul Dudley White exploded the myth that exercise would cause heart attacks. He pointed out that the heart is a muscle that needs exercise. Previously, wives at the country club had warned their husbands to get off the court with the admonition, "Do you want to have a heart attack?" That whole philosophy changed dramatically in the 1950s and 1960s when the notion that exercise was fundamentally healthy became popular. The stage was set for the popularization of tennis.

The origin of tennis goes back a long way. Evidence suggests that around the year 1100 monks in France played an indoor game, which first involved only a ball and one's hand, then a wrapped hand, then a glove and a *batoir* or bat. Finally a solid racquet was introduced, resulting in a game that was probably a combination of how tennis and squash are played today. Around 1500 the racquet evolved to a point that strings were added. However, the game was still played indoors, and many variations existed in the rules of the game and how it was played.

The original outdoor tennis—or lawn tennis—was invented in 1874, and the early court was in the shape of an hourglass, with the narrow part of the court at the net, which was somewhat higher than the present-day net. Players dressed in white or cream colored clothing. Men wore slacks and women wore long dresses, which eventually graduated into skirts.

In 1934, Henry E. "Bunny" Austin broke the dress code by wearing shorts at Wimbledon. Although Austin never reached the pinnacle of success as a great player, he always managed to play well on the Davis Cup team for Great Britain. In 1933, he and Fred Perry won the cup for Great Britain by defeating France in the final match, the first of four consecutive victories, never to be achieved again. Because Bunny Austin was such a strong competitor, the staid British officials were reluctant to protest when their star showed up on the tennis court one day wearing shorts.

For the next fifty or so years, players continued to use the traditional white on the pro tour with occasional exceptions—such as the matches played on the Jack Kramer Tour in the early 1950s when Gorgeous Gussy Moran became famous for her colorful short skirts and lace panties.

Even today at many of the older country clubs and tennis clubs, the white-only rule of clothing prevails. Though I do not consider myself a strong traditionalist, I have always encouraged white clothes at the St.

Albans Tennis Club. We allow an exception for warm-up gear. But in my view, there is still something satisfying about looking out over the St. Alban's courts and seeing everyone dressed in white.

Scoring has also changed in tennis. Prior to the 1950s, the scoring system required the winner of a set to win by two games. Many sets that ended in a 6–6 tie went on for hours, ending up 28–26, or 32–30, or even longer, until somebody got ahead by two games.

The scoring transformation was largely the result of a system devised by James Van Alen. Jimmy came to Washington during the Eisenhower years. He had raised a fairly sizeable sum of money for the president's election campaign and was rewarded with a rather insignificant position as chairman of the Selective Service Appeals Board, which required virtually no work. Van Alen was descended from one of the wealthiest families in the country, and his mother's home in Newport was one of the truly great American castles.

Jimmy and I played regularly at the Sheraton Park courts during the time that I was running the program there. He repeatedly told me that of the many pros who had instructed him I was the only one who taught him how to hit a forehand correctly. At the start of every lesson he would buy a dozen new balls, and at the end of every lesson, he would pay with large-denomination bills. It was always a fun experience, except that I had to listen to him expound upon what many considered to be a crazy scoring system that this eccentric millionaire was proposing.

Sometime later Jack Kramer and his traveling troupe came to Washington to play at the old Uline Arena in northeast Washington, and Kramer and Lew Hoad agreed to set aside time to test out the new scoring system with van Alen. The system was called VASSS (van Alen Streamlined Scoring System), and the inventor showed up with a handmade scorecard to record the play. Jimmy and I used the scorecard and kept score together. I doubt if anyone at the time, except Jimmy van Alen, held out any hope that his scoring system would be adopted. But by 1970 it had been accepted by the United States Tennis Association and was used not only in the United States but throughout the world. And I am the first to admit that the VASSS tie-breaking rule has had a far-reaching, positive effect upon the game, adding excitement and reducing the duration of matches.

Tennis has changed even more dramatically since the early 1980s. White is no longer the dress code for tournament play among professionals,* and the game itself has become more athletic and aggressive—for both men and women.

SPORTSMANSHIP

As anyone who has played tennis knows, the game has zero tolerance for cheaters. My take on cheating is this:

*Exceptions include tournaments played at Wimbledon.

I grew up in the old school where a player could cheat on his wife, steal large sums of money, be cruel to his dog, and use gamesmanship; but all these sins—as bad as they are—were forgivable. Abusing the trust of the honor system in tennis was not. Bearing an illegitimate child in a puritanical culture did not match the stigma that would accompany one who went through life as a cheater in tennis.

A person may be kind to his or her mother, a regular churchgoer, and a generous donor to charity; but if that person makes bad line calls consistently, in my view the player is fated to spend an eternity in tennis purgatory after enduring a lifetime of well-deserved scorn and ostracism from fellow racqueteers.

Often the habit of cheating originates with parents, or even at times with tennis coaches. One of the problems with tennis today is that it is notorious for encouraging a win-at-all-costs mentality among parents, an attitude which in many instances is detrimental to their children's careers and, even worse, their character.

It has always appalled me to observe the willingness of so many parents and coaches to ignore or even at times to support their charges in calling close calls to their own advantage. My experience has been that if the foe across the net is inclined to cheat and the parents' value system prizes winning above all else, that person's parents or coach usually support the bad calls. Often the person's opponent is intimidated into defeat.

As a matter of fact, the parents themselves sometimes outdo players and coaches in corner cutting. A parent of a promising young player volunteered to handle the draw for a minor tournament. Although a draw should be conducted in public, this parent retreated to a private room and arranged to put his son in one bracket while concentrating all the other good players in the other bracket so that his son would not have to meet a strong opponent until the finals. This is not an unusual occurrence and also falls into the category of bad sportsmanship, which is an extremely poor example for children.

When courts are concentrated in a contiguous area, a knowledgeable coach has the ability to watch six matches simultaneously. A player who habitually cheats cannot go undetected by a competent professional for very long. While many coaches discipline players for racquet throwing, obscenities, or temper tantrums during emotional matches, I have rarely seen a coach call down his charge because of cheating. Many coaches look the other way when one of their players touches the net and should have awarded the point to his opponent. After all they, too, have much to lose, because professional associations usually only honor coaches whose teams have a winning season.

With such misguided ideas about sportsmanship, it is no wonder that young people are getting mixed messages about ethics. A coach, for example, might juggle the lineup. Instead of matching the number-one player against the best player on the opposite team, when he knows that there is no conceivable way his player can win, he moves the worst player into the top position as a sacrificial lamb and then pushes everyone down one place. In my view, this is a form of cheating. Yet coaches often do it and the entire team knows of this unethical act. When this happens, however, rarely do parents complain that their children are being exposed to poor sportsmanship. In such situations more is at stake than the outcome of a tennis match. Players get the message that it is okay to cheat. If it pays to cheat in tennis tournaments, then it probably pays in other pursuits as well. Tennis should be a game that builds honesty and character in part precisely because until one reaches a certain level, players are their own umpires. Each player, or in the case of doubles each pair, must rely on the integrity of his or her opponent.

Over the years, I have seen the tennis honor system deteriorate, not just among youngsters and students. At the St. Albans Tennis Club I have observed on numerous occasions two old codgers, well-known in Washington and nationally for their involvement in public life, who consistently called shots in their own favor when it was obvious to me that they were wrong. This particular pair is infamous for their flagrantly wrong calls against each other, but they are not the only players who display such behavior. Not surprisingly, each of these men has been identified with unsavory episodes in his professional life as well.

Another element of sportsmanship became readily apparent when tennis began being covered on national television. This falls into the category of what I would call boorish behavior. Two chief culprits were John McEnroe and Jimmy Connors, whose behavior—thanks to television—was disseminated throughout the world.

Prior to the age of tennis television, tennis enjoyed a special cachet in the public mind. It might be okay for a coach such as Bobby Knight at the University of Indiana to catapult a chair across the basketball court or a football coach like Woody Hayes at Ohio State to grab an opposing player and shake his teeth loose from his gums; but this kind of behavior was not part of tennis. Tennis was supposed to be a gentleman's sport, a concept that seemed to disappear with the tennis performances of John McEnroe and Jimmy Connors on television.

Now, there is something to be said in defense of McEnroe's outrageous behavior. In the first place, his frequent and needlessly profane reaction to line calls was sometimes justified. McEnroe had extremely keen vision, which was one of the reasons why he became a world champion. The umpires who call the lines at big-time tournaments are generally ordinary club players with no better than normal eyesight, often not as good as that of the players. Also, the tennis stakes have become much higher. Agents, clubs, sponsors, officials, and sporting good manufacturers have turned tennis into a very big business. A couple of bad line calls could send a McEnroe or a Connors, or earlier, an Ilie Nastase—who was the inventor of the tennis temper tantrum—to the sidelines, deprived of a championship purse and the considerably more lucrative product endorsement money that comes with it.

Therefore it's understandable why these players protest calls they think are wrong. In this respect, tennis has become more like baseball and other professional sports. A baseball player, for example, who glares at an umpire after a strike call where the ball clearly missed the plate, is commonplace, as is a basketball star protesting a foul he didn't commit. We do not consider this inappropriate behavior. The tennis player, however, is supposed to be cut from different cloth. The fact is, however, that tennis players are probably no better or worse than anyone else, though custom in the past has led to more "gentlemanly" behavior.

Of course, long before John McEnroe's outlandish antics were regularly beamed around the globe, an unknown, but assuredly large number of players, routinely threw their racquets, whacked their balls over fences, and cursed and screamed about bad calls, their own poor play, or their opponent's habit of repeatedly acing or passing them. I remember once watching some high school players in a highly contested tournament. The scream emanating from the courts was blood curdling mixed with some minor profanity. The person sitting next to me was shocked. That was some years ago. People are not shocked by that kind of behavior today.

It is ironic that some people who insist on proper behavior on the tennis court do not practice such behavior in their own business or professional lives. One incident that sticks in my mind involved a high-ranking Nixon administration official, who lamented the conduct of the younger generation as he watched a private school's tennis tournament that involved considerable swearing and generally poor sportsmanship. This person frequently expressed his displeasure at what he was seeing and hearing. He exclaimed that such conduct portended doom for the country when the younger generation playing tennis took charge. The administration official, however, was not without his faults. He and his associates at the time were participating in a White House conspiracy to cover the Nixon administration's involvement in the burglary and dirty tricks campaign that came to be known as Watergate. He never sensed the irony that at the same time he was criticizing the young tennis players for their boorish behavior, he was compiling for Nixon a list of Jews in the Bureau of Labor Statistics who the president thought were manipulating economic data to make the administration look bad.

Other types of attitudes in tennis in addition to cheating, boorish behavior, and altering the lineups, fall into the category of bad sportsmanship. In the early 1950s the Woodmont Club, where I worked at the time, decided to open its facilities for a day to wounded Korean War veterans, many of them hospitalized at the Bethesda Naval and Walter Reed Army Hospitals. Those who were able were encouraged to play golf, tennis, or shuffleboard, or to swim or go fishing. For those less active, professional athletes and entertainers were ready to perform. Vice President Nixon spoke a few words. Food, prizes, and souvenirs abounded. As everybody departed at the end of the day, official club members were deeply moved by the experience and were teary eyed, as were many of the veterans, some of whom were amputees.

My role in this endeavor was to direct the tennis exhibition, which included some informal free play as well as some competitive tennis. In 1953 I set up an exhibition in which I was to play with Pauline Betz Addie and Clark Taylor, an area professional and formerly a top intercollegiate player. For the fourth player I had promised to get someone of considerable stature in the tennis world. The man I chose had been on the Davis Cup team for the United States and had won numerous national tournaments. I thought he would be something of an inspiration to many of the handicapped participants since he himself suffered from a chronic ailment.

Pauline almost had to cancel because her husband was in the hospital, but she rose to the occasion and not only showed up but put on a superlative display of tennis, as was customary for her. But the former Davis Cup champion performed miserably. Worse, he was not the least bit gracious toward the servicemen guests. And although a number of participants in the program refused to take expense money for their appearances, he accepted his plane fare, which was to be expected. We also agreed to pick him up at the airport and to pay him an additional $100 for expenses. He was furious, demanding that we pay him an extra $50 stating that he would usually receive "one and a half" for appearing in a tennis exhibition. The irony was that he was the amateur and the rest of us—who were receiving no compensation whatsoever—were the professionals. This kind of behavior also falls into the category of what I would call poor sportsmanship.

PUTTING TOO MUCH EMPHASIS ON WINNING

One of the reasons for poor sportsmanship, in my view, is that too much emphasis is placed on winning. Of course, people prefer to win. That's the point of competition. But when winning becomes the only thing, matters get out of hand. As a tournament player, I loved competition, although I often wondered if it was worth it, given the stress associated with competing day in and day out, especially when you get to the fifth set on a day when the temperature hits a hundred degrees.

However, competition, especially at a high level, is not for everyone. Most players, the vast majority, are those who play tennis simply for the enjoyment of the game. The goal of a good coach, therefore, is to give enough instruction to enable the pupil to enjoy the sport and to instill a love of the game in that person without taking away the fun.

The problem is that both coaches and parents often ruin it for their pupils. Mom and Pop enjoy the vicarious feelings of producing a champion, while coaches are on an ego trip for their own record. Schools stress their excellence by touting their athletic achievements, often above their academic achievements.

When a high school reporter once came to me for an interview about the tennis program at St. Albans School, the first questions he asked was, "What is your win/loss record?" I don't keep such silly records anyway, but I responded with "Two Rhodes Scholars." My goal has been to see that in the future, the youngsters I have taught tennis to will be playing for the physical and mental health associated with the sport, instead of sitting in front of a TV with a six-pack of beer watching others participate.

TOO MUCH PRESSURE

Another threat to the sport of tennis involves the pressure now associated with the game, especially at the higher levels of competition. Our society seems to be obsessed with sports and often emphasizes sports over academics. For example, very few teachers appear on TV or have newspaper articles written about them while the winning coach is showered with attention. This encourages coaches to put greater emphasis on winning. Their allies, of course, are the parents of the better athletes, who are seeking the rewards, scholarships, and ultimately the earnings that accrue to them and their offspring. Just as President Eisenhower warned of the military-industrial complex, a small but determined alliance of coaches and parents who are starting to dominate schools and institutions present a danger to the sport. I call this coalition "the institutional-sports complex."

The pressure to win and be successful is responsible for most of the abuses in tennis. Kids are being driven by coaches who feel their sport is the main thing in life. Practices often go on too long, and while the rest of the school may be given a day off during a holiday, athletic teams are usually required to practice. As a result, family life often suffers as the child tries to study, have dinner with family, and still lead a life that is manageable. It is quite a balancing act.

In some cases, young people are intimidated into playing a sport, especially if they have talent. On the other hand, the unathletic child, who may need the sport the most in order to learn life skills for later use in life, is often neglected. In the case of tennis, this child is often left out because courts and teaching time are reserved for the varsity and the students with more promising athletic ability.

The bottom line, in my view, is that competitive sports are whirling out of control with far too much pressure than is healthy. Sports need to be put back into perspective.

MONEY UNDER THE TABLE

In the tennis "extended family," not much is said about appearance money for stars. Appearance money is given to top players simply for showing up for a tournament. This is one of tennis's dirty little secrets. A good bit of fanfare arose not too long ago about Steffi Graf's father reportedly collecting cash appearance fees for a 1992 tournament from the tournament director. Ion Tiriac, the feisty Romanian, filed a civil lawsuit against Graf's father for return of the fee when Graf withdrew because of an injury. This action, coming after several years in which no tax returns had been filed for Graf, sparked an inquiry by German tax officials. Eventually, after a broad examination of Graf's earnings and tax filings, Steffi's father was found guilty of tax evasion and spent time in jail in Germany.

Apparently getting money under the table in addition to prize money is actually legal as long as you pay taxes on it. Even though the Women's Tennis Association theoretically doesn't allow players to accept this kind of bonus, they have not prohibited the practice. One problem of paying money under the table is that it leaves less money to go around at the end of the day to support some of the charities that in many instances tournament proceeds are intended to serve.

Some tennis charities often find themselves having less money than anticipated for their charitable work, due to having to pay the top players to show up. Although legal, I believe the practice is unethical. The problem is that top players are able to choose among tournaments running concurrently, and tournament organizers need some incentive to attract the stronger players. This is another example of what is wrong with contemporary tennis.

Usually the money is given without any guarantee of performance. If the named player loses in the first round, he or she gets the cash. In some cases, however, athletes rise to the occasion. Several years ago while playing in Washington, Andre Agassi, who, of course, was one of the big-name attractions, lost in the first round and I heard he returned the appearance fee, which showed a touch of class.

ELITISM IN TENNIS

In the early days of tennis, tournaments were dominated by the upper class. Well-known family names dominated the draw sheets. The democratization of tennis began in the 1950s and increased all the way into the 1980s. This has been a good trend, opening up tennis to people who previously have been excluded, and in fact it has transformed the game. Unfortunately, some signs suggest that the democratization might be coming to an end and that tennis may be returning to the status of an elitist sport. This is especially true in regions of the country where it is not possible to play year-round outdoor tennis.

The problem, of course, is money and access to facilities. Indoor tennis time and coaching cost money, not to mention the expense associated with full-time, year-round tennis programs and tennis schools. It is not unusual today for children to be chauffeured from court to court, given access to participating pros for endless hours, sent off to tournaments around the country, often with their own pros and sometimes with their trainers and psychologists, and for parents to spend huge amounts of money to make their children competitive. A talented athlete living in the inner-city, often in a situation where the family has trouble scraping together enough money to put food on the table, certainly is not able to buy expensive racquets and to obtain the coaching and court time required to become competitive. Playing a lot and playing with other good players is critical to success in tennis.

The United States Tennis Association (USTA) has been involved for a number of years in fostering a development program for inner-city children. But because of limited resources, they cannot provide the attention that so many children from wealthy families are receiving. If this trend continues, it will be increasingly difficult for inner-city kids to develop into strong competitive players. It is no wonder that the top tennis players in the country today generally are from the upper socioeconomic strata.

And competitiveness is not all that important. Tennis is a sport that will last a lifetime. It is critical to open up the sport to people who want to play on a recreational basis and to encourage a love for the game that will persist and promote healthy adult lifestyles. Children from lower-income and minority families should not be deprived of this opportunity. While the programs sponsored by the USTA are important, they are not nearly enough.

In Washington, the outreach effort sponsored by the Washington Tennis and Education Foundation is a positive trend. The foundation hosts a major tournament, usually held in the late summer, the proceeds of which are donated to help disadvantaged children. With a tireless effort on the part of several board members, the foundation developed a new tennis center with a stadium holding 7,500 people. Each year the tournament attracts many of the nation's finest tennis players and championship trophies have gone to the likes of Andre Agassi, Arthur Ashe, Ken Rosewall, Ivan Lendl, and Harold Solomon. The net proceeds are used for both academic tutorial work and tennis training, often providing college admission assistance and scholarships for the most deserving young players. Over $1 million was provided for such purposes in 2002.

PROFESSIONAL VOLUNTEERS

Volunteerism has had a very positive impact on tennis. Some of the best tennis officials have given their valuable time devoting countless hours to such matters as bringing the sport to inner-city children, promoting tennis, running tournaments, and generally making the largely volunteer effort run. I have seen presidential advisers and cabinet level officials taking the time to meet and discuss board policy for these various nonprofit organizations. Some of these unpaid board members would be the envy of any major United States corporation.

On the other hand, I have seen disasters caused by what I call the "professional volunteer." This individual religiously attends every meeting of the organization. At election time, he or she will invariably volunteer for the thankless job of secretary. The only catch is that eventually many of these people end up with the job of vice president of the organization, and just as Mondays follow Sundays, the vice presidents then become presidents. Like the Peter Principle, where one gets promoted until he or she reaches a point of incompetence for that job, professional volunteerism often produces poor leadership. Hereafter this shall be known as the "Allie Principle."

Promotion, unfortunately, doesn't stop at the local level. The local volunteer president then goes on to regional and national offices where in many instances he or she is totally inept and even less qualified. It is the title that is thought to be prestigious, implying that its holder is prominent. The problem is that, more often than not, the person is incompetent. The Allie Principle states that volunteerism becomes counterproductive and sometimes detrimental when professional volunteers get to run the show when their only qualification is a driver's license (had they not started off driving their kids to tennis practice, they never would have gotten started), and their only intent is to build a resume. This is a form of graduated incompetence that we permit in this democratic society, not only for tennis programs, but for many nonprofit corporations. Because the truly qualified individuals are often too busy or not interested, the field is open for people who have more time on their hands than is good for them.

The problem is made worse when the bad eggs who have become officers and leaders in these organizations cannot be removed because of the "good old boy" system. They scratch each other's backs and are dependent on each other to remain in power. "Don't rock the boat" and "cooperate to graduate" often seem to be the code, which ultimately does not work to anyone's advantage.

The United States Tennis Association has had a great number of fine and excellent volunteers, but it also has showcases of the Allie Principle. For example, in choosing teams for international competition—and I have been on five of them—the best players are not always selected. For the most part, the team captains have done as well as the players, but on several occasions I have seen some who are a disgrace to the United States before a world audience, due to favoritism.

We should honor those who devote their time to various activities, spend countless hours working behind the scenes, and are responsible for the success of our recreational and social programs. They deserve the recognition. But these organizations should be more selective in picking their leaders, whether it be the Little League, the PTA, political organizations, athletic associations, cultural groups, social clubs, educational enclaves, or schools and universities.

INDIVIDUAL VERSUS TEAM PLAY

One of the core elements of tennis that originally attracted me to the sport was its focus on the competition between individuals rather than between teams. I liked the idea that my success or failure on any given day would be determined mainly by my own personal performance, and not by the performance of my teammates. By and large I was likely to win or lose depending on how well I played (though, of course, the performance of my opponent or doubles partner could certainly influence the outcome.)

As I grew older and understood the game better I recognized that this individuality of play carried with it a burden for acknowledging and adhering voluntarily to the rules and for self-policing. If I tried to bend the rules in day-to-day play, I knew I'd regret it once I was in competition, with umpires and linesmen officiating. For young people, as I have suggested earlier, this recognition helps build character and instill the values of honesty and forthrightness.

While participation in team sports can certainly be beneficial for many youngsters, it has a downside that is frequently overlooked. It often makes players worry unduly about how they fit in with the team and how they are regarded by their teammates. In some youngsters this concern outweighs their respect for the rules and induces them to cut corners.

Over the years I have found that one often sees a parallel to this tendency in adult life. With the virtues of being a team player widely touted, whether in business or in public affairs, they can be carried too far. Grown men and women, while focusing on their approval within the team, lose sight of the key elements of the sport itself. After reading every day about examples of persons who demonstrated this tendency I got fired up enough about this issue some years ago to submit a column to *The Washington Post* that was published in August 1987 under the heading of "When Team Play Is Cheating: Sports Too Often Teach Us to Sacrifice Honor for Success." Here, in part, is what I said:

> Sports has long provided us with allegories that help us understand the greater game of life—its temptations, tribulations, and triumphs. But now sports may be teaching us, and especially our young, a terribly wrong lesson. . . .
>
> We constantly hear statesmen and politicians expound on the merits of being a team player. Do they mean that a team player who lies and cheats to further the team is performing an honorable duty? Should a team player who knows of a

> crime keep quiet because it is his own team that is guilty? Should whistle-blowers be harassed because they have "ratted" on the team instead of going along with its corruption or inefficiency? This is an age of wrongdoing: Watergate, Mylai, corporate scandals, defense overcharges, environmental crimes, stock-market manipulation, the Iran-contra disaster. How many of those involved in these scandals justified themselves as team players?

Bob McNamara, in both his book *In Retrospect* (1995) and the recent documentary film *Fog of War* (2003), acknowledges the close link between loyalty and team play and how easy it is to confuse dissenting opinion with disloyalty. I think this goes a long way toward explaining how a man of such high intelligence and integrity who is kind, courteous, considerate, and compassionate could have become so embroiled in the conduct of the Vietnam War.

Despite the challenges that tennis faces today, it continues to be a great sport. The biggest challenges confronting tennis are shared by many other sports. And many of the problems affecting tennis are rooted in broader social conditions. Furthermore, many of these problems simply boil down to plain old human frailty. At the same time, in order for tennis to continue to be the great sport that it is, those of us who love the game must exercise diligence and address the excesses in the sport when they arise.

Sphairistike or Lawn Tennis
The first book on lawn tennis
46 pages, very rare
WALTER WINGFIELD
1873 7 3/8" x 4 7/8" x 1/8"

CHAPTER 6

Tennis Antiquity and Aesthetics

After touring our home, a recent visitor made the comment, "You know, Allie, for an art museum, this is actually a fairly comfortable place to live."

Our house is perched upon a wooded hill several hundred feet high, overlooking the Potomac River about three miles upstream from the heart of Washington. There is a large picture window across from the front door, so the first thing a person sees when opening the door is an unobstructed view of the Potomac. As breathtaking as this view is—and I never tire of it—the view is not what makes the house special. What makes the house special is that it houses my collection of tennis antiquities and tennis-inspired art, the largest private collection of its type in the world.

During the majority of my adult life I have spent considerable time tracking down and purchasing tennis objects of all types, and this pursuit has been something of an obsession. It's an eclectic collection, which I wanted to have both for my own enjoyment and to be able to pass along to my children. The collection involves articles that have either artistic or historical value, all with a racquet motif. The objects date back as far as the pre-Columbian period and go through the Art Deco period, and include paintings, prints, bronzes, ceramics, glass, textiles, silver, toys, games, watches, clocks, jewelry, books, posters, racquets, tiles, porcelains, and many other items. Many of them adorn the walls and bookcases throughout every room in my house. The majority, however, are stored away for lack of wall space.

Many of the items relate to the evolution of the sport of tennis. When Major Walter Wingfield invented the game of lawn tennis in 1873–74, after starting the Cordon Rouge Society in England, he packaged a set of racquets, a net, and balls into a wooden box and gave the game the unpronounceable title of "Sphairistike" after the Greek word with the root meaning "sphere" or "ball game." The sets did not sell very well, so with an eye for business the major decided to tone the name down and he pasted a new label on the box calling the game "lawn tennis." The sport took off immediately.

Actually, the roots of tennis go back many centuries under such names as "real tennis" or "royal tennis," or "court tennis," or in French, "*jeu de paume*." The French game originated from the "game of the palm" or hand ball, which then took on different forms such as bindings on the hand and eventually racquets. In fact, few people who have marveled at the art displayed at the Paris museum called Jeu de Paume realize that the building was originally a tennis court, hence its name. Of course, the early game was restricted to a very small number of aristocrats, who had the luxury of playing in the buildings.

In 1599, Shakespeare in *King Henry V* described the "Dauphin" tennis incident of 1414, which was recreated on film not too long ago. The game of tennis was referenced earlier, in the year 1245, at Rouen where there were ecclesiastical restrictions on tennis. One king found that his soldiers were spending so much time on the tennis court that they were neglecting their archery practice. He forbade the playing of tennis for all people except royalty.

The idea for my collection can be attributed to a visit by Larry Gichner. He came from a prominent Washington family that had prospered in various industries such as steel and roofing for major D.C. buildings. Larry had a hobby of collecting erotica, a hobby that caused him some trouble with the legal establishment in staid Washington. In addition to erotic folk art, he also owned some finer pieces by famous artists who at the time were unable to publicly display them because of their controversial content.

At one point Larry was arrested and faced a jail sentence for what the prosecutors called "the dirty pictures" in his home. A good lawyer got him off, but in order to maintain his collection, he satisfied the lawmakers of the District of Columbia by transferring his collection to a newly formed foundation. The artwork owned by the foundation was displayed in the Gichner home, which was located across from the Washington National Cathedral not far from the bishop's office. As a bona fide educational foundation, the small gallery was open for selective visits, and I was invited once along with a group of psychiatrists to view the collection. I was very impressed.

Not long after that, in 1962, Larry Gichner paid a visit to the St. Albans courts with three pictures. These were not the erotic photos in his house but rather snapshots of an 1884 Fourth of July family picnic. Some of the participants were holding tennis racquets. They were marvelous vintage shots that would make interesting decorations for an otherwise dull tennis shop, so I bought them.

Larry asked if I would be interested in anything else relating to tennis. Of course, I was. He placed an ad in an antique trade journal and was able to supply me with a number of other pieces of tennis artwork. At one point he mentioned that a George Bellows oil painting of a tennis scene at Newport might be available, but it would cost about $1,800. I couldn't afford it, which was unfortunate because it was later donated by Paul Mellon to the National Gallery of Art and is probably today valued at several million dollars. I did, however, buy a pair of Newport prints by Bellows, which became a later addition to my budding collection.

Collecting can be an addiction. One spends innumerable hours chasing down items by going to antique shows, shops, and auctions, and by pursuing every lead. It gets to be a hunt with a chase that eventually leads to the capture. As one becomes more mature and sophisticated, one's tastes change toward only the most rare, beautiful, and ancient objects. My collection now totals more than fifteen hundred pieces and Peggy has suggested that our residence may be taking on too much of my personality.

One prominent piece in the collection is a set of two large stained glass windows that came from a spa built in the Adirondacks between 1870 and 1875, depicting a woman in pre-Raphaelite style holding a tennis racquet. These windows are probably the oldest stained glass of their type with a tennis scene. The architect who was restoring the Newport Hall of Fame Tennis Museum was desperate to get one of the windows for placement at the entrance of the museum. Not long after I acquired these windows, a delegation of women representing the Newport Tennis Museum journeyed to Washington to try to convince me that I should donate them to the historic building that had been designed by Stanford White in 1881 during the start of the era of lavish living there.

After a discussion with my estate lawyer, I decided that it would be unfair to my heirs to give away the windows but I did offer to let the museum borrow them free of charge for a couple of years. Eventually I agreed to allow a photograph of the stained glass to be blown up to life size. The photograph was properly lighted so that it resembled the glass, and it now hangs at the top of the stairs leading to the Tennis Hall of Fame.

My collection includes just about anything and everything you can find with a racquet on it. I still collect and search things out by attending antique shows, stopping at antique shops, and buying at auctions and from dealers. I ask if they have anything with a tennis motif, and with a trained eye quickly size it up. Some of my best objects have come from dealers who had things back in their warehouse or storeroom or at their home. This technique has proven especially useful in the famous flea markets in London and Paris. My collection also contains the first book on tennis, by Scaino, written in 1555, and the first book on lawn tennis from 1874, both extremely rare. I also have some of the earliest tennis illustrations dating back to the early 1500s.

In France, my usual opening was, "*objects avec motif du tennis*?" It generally worked except in one shop in Paris where a proprietor nodded that he did have something for me. As he walked over to a series of flat files, I figured he would have some useless old prints, but I agreed to look at them anyway. He brought out the first print and I drew a complete blank. I could see no racquet at all and was quite perplexed. Another graphic came out and I frowned at this one also, with a puzzled look on my face. At this point, typical of many Parisians who are intolerant of Americans, he exclaimed as if I couldn't tell what was in the pictures. "Ici penis," he exclaimed, "ici penis!" I couldn't keep myself from laughing to the point of convulsion, and wildly swung my arms in mock forehands and backhands, yelling, "Tennis! Tennis! Not penis!"

If Larry Gichner had still been alive, I would have bought the dealer's print as a gift for him in appreciation for starting me off on the tennis collection.

Occasionally I loan some of the items to museums or organizations. Because lawn tennis came to the United States via Bermuda in 1874 when Mary Outerbridge allegedly brought back the tennis equipment to Staten Island, I sent up about 120 antique items to a small museum there in 1997 for a show. But most of the time I have intimate small group shows at my home, where the audience seems astounded that such a collection even exists. It is an unusual way to entertain, but the guests seem to enjoy it as something special. I now realize that because of its size and value, I should not allow the collection to be split up. I hope to see it go to a university with a good art department and one that has a good tennis program with spacious facilities. Or it could go to a corporate headquarters or a museum such as the one in Newport.

I also find tennis itself an exercise in aesthetics. Played correctly, it is thrilling and beautiful to watch. The strokes are beautiful in their simplicity. Overdone, however, tennis strokes can show extraneous qualities, like a second-rate Arthur Murray dance pupil. Likewise, when not sufficiently mastered, the strokes can look stilted and stiff.

A worthy professional can sense that efficiency and beauty go hand in hand, and a good tennis game should be aesthetically pleasing to watch. Often I find it painful to watch a lovely creative woman walk through the gates of the tennis courts poised and self-confident, only to display a Jekyll and Hyde appearance when she starts playing tennis, using strokes that belong to a complete clod. However, with proper coaching I believe the clumsiest person can achieve gracefulness though this is only possible if it is a deliberate goal.With beauty in mind and the belief that tennis is an art form, I consider teaching grace in tennis as one of my missions in life.

This attitude applies not only to teaching but also to the environment in which tennis is played. At St. Albans, for example, for years the clubhouse was the butt of jokes, and rightly so, because it consisted of a small hut resembling an outhouse. My secretary and shop manager were stationed there and received calls from various members of the cabinet, senators, congressmen and others of great influence. It did not seem an appropriate environment for managing a tennis club.

So we concluded that a new tennis house should be built compact enough to fit into a small area and consistent with the architectural styles found elsewhere on the grounds of the Washington National Cathedral. We felt the new tennis shop should be unobtrusive and blend in with the buildings around it. I believed it also should have some charm.

With this goal in mind, in 1969 I recommended the young architectural firm of Hartman Cox. Warren Cox was a fair tennis player, who played tennis in high school and later studied architecture at Yale. With the help of George Hartman he dug into the task. The result was a prize-winning structure, which won the Louis Sullivan Award of the International Union of Bricklayers for preeminent architecture. The building won several other awards. Years later practicing architects still study the St. Albans Tennis Club along with the Renwick Gallery and other famous Washington buildings.

I believe that tennis prizes should not be ugly, corny pieces of gilt, as is often the case with trophies in various sports. Often the smaller and less significant tournaments have the larger and more garish trophies.

One year I had a sculptor design ceramic trophies for the annual club tournament. Another year I commissioned my pupil, Sam Gilliam, to make a print to use as a prize. This took a lot of financial maneuvering, since Sam has shown at major galleries throughout the world, though I later learned that this engagement was actually his first paid commission. Also, Lou Stovall, reputedly the finest silk screen artist in the nation and also a pupil of mine and close friend of Gilliam's, did the printing. The print was officially unveiled at the awards party where it met with enthusiastic acclaim. Finalists in all events were given signed prints, which the artist limited to sixty.

As a youngster, I played baseball for years but never really became a fan of the game. The late Shirley Povich, renowned as a sports writer, once told me that he saw similarities between baseball and ballet. I decided to watch some games on television to see what he meant. The infield double play, where the ball goes to second base and then to the first baseman starts to take on greater significance when seen in the context of art and dance. I could see the beauty in it, as well as the charm of a leaping catch in the outfield. As a result, I found modern dance with its natural movements much more satisfying than certain movements in classical ballet where the knees and feet seem to go in the wrong direction, causing what seems to me to be a rather awkward situation.

It is important to realize that if an individual locks his or her knees and turns from the waist, the body can go only ninety degrees in each direction, or halfway around. Yet when the knees are relaxed, the body can swing around a full 360 degrees. The grace of a tennis player—or for that matter a golfer or a baseball player—is enhanced by the relaxed motion of the back leg and knee, which naturally allows the waist and shoulders to rotate without tearing the muscles. To see a block of freshly mowed grass courts with the players dressed in the traditional white is a bewitching aesthetic sight, and this scene has been the subject of some of the best tennis art. Somehow, certain players exude beauty through their stature, poise, fluid movements, and manners.

I often remind my female pupils of the old Ziegfield Follies in New York. Over the entrance was a sign that read, "Through these portals pass the most beautiful women in the world." I would then point to an archway leading to my teaching court and tell the women that through that portal pass the most *graceful* women in the world. "Now, bring that grace with you. Don't leave it on the other side of the entrance."

One of the most graceful women I have ever coached was Phyllis Dillon, wife of Douglas Dillon, then secretary of the treasury under President Kennedy. This woman struck me as very elegant, in both her style of tennis play and her general carriage. Her clothing and demeanor all added up to grace and what I thought was a classy style.

Another member with exceptional grace was Mary Louise Reid, whose husband Ogden "Browny" Reid came to Washington as a member of Congress from Westchester County, New York, after having served as ambassador to Israel. A male club member who had this magic grace and charm was John Lindsay, a member of the House of Representatives from the silk stocking district of New York before he became mayor of New York City.

Many of these beautiful people were born with a silver spoon in their mouth and were taught the social graces. But the truly elegant were genuinely sincere and were not phonies in any way. They went beyond the training by nannies and the fine schools and were fundamentally decent people.

Some of these people had also been exposed to the other side of life. A good example was Paul Moore. Before becoming Episcopal bishop of New York, he spent several years as Suffragan bishop of the Diocese of Washington, where he was an activist in the civil rights and peace movements. He and his wife Jenny, who bravely fought cancer before she died, had lived among the poor in a New Jersey ghetto. Jenny's book *The People of Second Street* described their experience beautifully. She believed that those eight years were the most rewarding of their careers. Paul and Jenny were definitely an example of grace and beauty.

Tray with tennis scene (two views)
Ceramic, English
ROSARIO
circa 1880 9" x 24"

CHAPTER 7

Reflections

When I picked up my first tennis racket, a wooden one, at the age of nine in 1927, I never would have dreamed that tennis would take me to courts in so many diverse places. These courts have been located in some of Washington's poorest neighborhoods, with broken glass and debris, and in the most beautiful Gardens of Eden on the planet. During the war I played on leveled anthills in the northern territory of Australia, makeshift courts in New Guinea, and in the semi-wilderness of the Philippines. I also have played on the beautifully landscaped grounds of the White House and on courts located on the grounds of the finest hotels in the world, such as the Greenbrier at White Sulphur Springs, where I won my first sectional collegiate championship. I have played on courts located at the governor's mansion in Punjab, India, and on the estates of the Rockefellers, Goulds, Mellons, and with the Astors, Morgans, Whitneys, DuPonts, and Rothschilds.

My tennis journeys have been far-flung. One of these courts was the private indoor court of the Soviet KGB. I practiced on this court when I won the Soviet singles and doubles championships just weeks before the dissolution of the Soviet Union in 1989. The finals of the International Tennis Federation World's Championship senior event on the center court at Kooyong in Melbourne, Australia, were memorable. I played another tournament in China, at their first senior championship where seniors players were allowed only to play doubles. Tennis gave me, literally, a chance to see the world.

Imagine a scenario where in the afterlife a tennis pro is being interviewed by St. Peter at the Pearly Gates. "And what did you do for humanity during your lengthy lifetime on earth?" asked St. Peter.

"I was a tennis pro."

"And what, pray tell, is tennis?"

"It's a sport where racquets are used to slam a rubber ball over an obstacle called a net and you have to keep the ball within specified boundaries."

"And what do you mean by racquets? Do they make loud noises?"

"No. When I first started playing they were long, oblong-shaped wooden frames with long handles. Holes were bored in the frame so that dried lamb intestines, or gut, could be tightly woven. Now they have large frames and are made with light, high-tech materials."

"What was the object of this foolishness?"

"Well," I replied, "if a player could knock the ball successfully back one more time than his or her opponent, the person was rewarded with points and eventually would win the game if that player was able to keep that up. Besides giving participants loads of exercise, fun, and sometimes grief, at times players who were the best at returning the ball became famous and rich beyond their wildest dreams. And they became role models for many little children and grown-up people."

"Where do you fit in during all this?"

"Well, I instructed thousands of people how to hit that little ball with more grace than they had before; and I instructed them how to play better by referring to basic principles involving mathematics, physics, rhythm and balance, and psychology."

"Is that all?" asked St. Peter.

"Well, I organized people in groups or clubs and even built places for the population to play, both when the weather was inclement and also when it was beautiful. And, though it's probably not all deserved, I have been given credit for being instrumental in getting a lot of people to take up the sport as a pastime."

I don't know that this will be good enough to get someone through the gates of heaven, but I hope so. And I can't help chuckling when I remember Canon Martin's remark that it was easier to get into heaven than to get into the St. Albans Tennis Club.

In addition to being a lover of the game and a devotee of sound tennis teaching, I have been a fierce competitor. I seem to play better when in competition and usually rise to the occasion. I remember once I had an opponent who went to the net and showed a beautiful barrage of volleys and a great overhead. Before the start of the set, he tried several serves which sped by me or would kick with a wide angle. He never made a mistake. At this point I was ready to leave the court, fearing that I was in for a tough day. We started the match, and the first game was close. He won that game. But after that, there was no match. Under pressure he could not score. That is a situation, however, that I thrive in. There is more to tennis than just athletic ability. Drive, self-confidence, and the desire to win are all key factors. Winning the warm-up does not count.

I have often wondered why a soloist musician tends to get all the praise while thousands of musicians, who are also exceptionally fine performers, are working in the symphony orchestras as unknowns. Is there a great difference in their playing abilities? What is the difference between them? Why does one star performer receive all the accolades and the huge monetary rewards, while others who are almost as good do not excel? My answer is that something in the human heart is transformed by what is called drive or the desire to win. That something special is what makes a difference.

As I look back on these years, I try to analyze the motives that have inspired me to be a strong competitor and to try to achieve as much as I can. I have won many world championships and have acquired what is considered by some to be the finest collection of tennis antiquities in the world. I am internationally known as a tennis teacher and created one of the most prestigious tennis clubs in the world.

I am quite certain that my marriage has been central to my achievements. Peggy came from a different stratum of society than I did. She came from a family of upper-class achievers and intellectuals, and she was a constant victim of pressure. Her family was close knit, and she tried hard to please them. However, she was constantly reminded by her family of her association with insignificant social elements, which I believed included me. When I worked at the Woodmont Country Club, she was somewhat troubled because she felt that the members of the club looked upon me as part of the "hired help." I demanded that my family and I be given all the privileges of club membership so that I would not be thought of as a second-class citizen, though at the time it was customary in many clubs for pros to be prohibited from eating in the main dining room. For me this was unacceptable.

Peg's sisters were both married to high achievers, men whom I admired and with whom I enjoyed excellent relationships. Her sister Barbara's husband, Albert Rosenthal, achieved fame in the legal profession, graduating as the number-one student at Harvard Law School and serving as president of the Law Review. He clerked for Justice Felix Frankfurter and later became Dean of the Columbia School of Law.

Her other sister, Marjorie, was widowed early and passed the California bar at the age of sixty-five. She was married to David Posner, who, after leaving the Federal Aviation Administration, had a very successful engineering career as head of supersonic and advanced design for North American Aircraft.

Peg's family exhibited a competitive attitude as well, which proclaimed "anything you can do, I can do better," or at least as well. Because of my own competitive spirit, I felt I had to prove to Peg and to her family that I was their equal and that with hard effort I, too, could excel. Tennis was one way that I could prove my worthiness. When I became dissatisfied winning local tournaments, set my sights on national and international titles, and went on to win a number of them.

Gun violence has been all too common in Washington over the years, a good number of shootings occurring simply because one person has "dissed" another person, or showed them disrespect. While taking such extreme action may be hard for some people to understand, I can understand it. I do not condone violence, but I know what it means to try to earn respect and feel like an outsider.

I have also been lucky to have had good health, which is especially important in a profession that requires so much energy and stamina. While I was never trained as present-day athletes are regarding their regimen and personal health, I have been careful of my food intake, having been a vegetarian since the age of nineteen. This practice, along with daily exercise and spending a lot of time outdoors, has probably made a difference. Another factor is my genes. Though my mother died young, my father was very active until the age of eighty-four. My brother, who is two years older than I am, played competitive tennis until the age of eighty-four. A third factor is modern medicine. At age seventy-eight my doctor discovered that I had blocked arteries, and I underwent quintuple bypass surgery, giving me the dubious honor of qualifying to play in the annual Bypass Open Tournament.

In addition to Peg, of course, I am grateful for my four children. My children are often questioned about their tennis, as people assume that they must be outstanding. While they all took lessons, participated in tennis clinics, and witnessed many tennis exhibitions, my policy was not to push them. Later in life, they told me that maybe I should have pushed them a little more.

The three boys, Kenneth, Frank and Frederick, played on championship high school tennis teams at Walt Whitman in Bethesda. Ken was at the top of his varsity tennis team at Syracuse University, where he spent ten years as an undergraduate, graduate, and law school student. His wife, Susie, is a social psychologist, and they have two boys, Daniel and Aaron.

Frank started with a tennis team at the University of Wisconsin but preferred to play social tennis instead. He continued his graduate study as a teaching assistant at the University of Pennsylvania. For a while, he taught tennis and coached the Madeira School team to an unbeaten season. He is now self-employed as a food broker and has been very successful. He also plays tennis at a club outside of Washington. His wife, Linda, works in the security business. Their two daughters, Alex and Mia, have played tennis and are talented artists.

Fred went off to the San Francisco Art Institute, where he earned bachelor's and master's degrees. That school has no athletic teams, except possibly frisbee, so his tennis reached a standstill at that point. After a hiatus of about fifteen years when he worked as a film maker, he joined the Mill Valley Tennis Club in California and started playing again. He now plays competitive tennis and asked me to play with him in a national father-and-son tournament not too many years ago. Some of the players expressed astonishment that he was playing with his old father instead of his young son. We did win a round, but then were creamed by one of the Bryan twins who was playing with his father. The Bryan twins are now playing on the pro circuit. Fred's two sons are divided in their interests. The younger one, Sam, is a strong athlete whose main sport is baseball. The other son, Max, is determined to succeed in theatre and graduated from the Tisch School at New York University.

Our daughter Kate is ten years younger than her oldest sibling. She has always preferred horses to tennis. When Peg and I were away on a trip, she got her older brother to drive her to Manassas, Virginia, where she bought an old horse, who was at times unmanageable. On another occasion two of my pupils, Hollis and Mary Chenery, invited Peg and me to a weekend at their country farm. Since they had a breeding farm, they suggested that Kate come along. Their horses included Riva Ridge and Secretariat, back-to-back Kentucky Derby winners in 1972 and 1973. They let Kate take another of their horses out on their track, and this little kid started to gallop away at full speed, almost giving her parents a nervous breakdown.

Kate and her husband, Mark, bought a horse, hoping that their daughter, Lea, also would ride, but Lea never was that interested in horses. She is well coordinated, however, and was on the varsity crew, lacrosse, and soccer teams at her high school in Washington, D.C. before going off to college at the University of Michigan. Once or twice a year she plays tennis and she has the ability to be a good player. Their son, Noah, plays sports, but is not competitive yet. Mark teaches English as a second language in the D.C. school system while Kate is a special education teacher at Washington's Duke Ellington School of the Arts. All of our children have the equivalent of at least a master's degree.

As active as I have been, I can't come close to the doings of my wife. Peg plays tennis twice a week, occasionally plays golf, belongs to three book clubs, and serves as a docent at two museums, the Hirshhorn and the National Museum of American Art, and leads tours of the art collection at Washington Reagan National Airport. She has ushered at the Arena Stage for many years and rarely misses any theater or dance group that performs in Washington. In addition, her travels have taken her to more than one hundred countries; it is rare when she is not abroad for four or five trips each year. Sometimes she accompanies me when I play in an interesting place. For other trips, she goes with one of her sisters or with tour groups, and she is especially fond of programs oriented towards the arts. Often I will pick a country in which to play a major tournament in order to entice her to accompany me, such as the Asian championship in Thailand, which permitted us visits to Cambodia, Myanmar, and Vietnam.

The game of tennis has been good to me. It has afforded me a rich and enduring lifestyle. I have met six presidents of the United States and have mingled with many of Washington's most powerful and most famous people. At the same time, I have taught tennis to some of Washington's most disadvantaged children and to inmates of mental hospitals. I have enjoyed playing around the world in the best and in the worst of conditions. I have come in contact with untold numbers of wonderful people, along with my share of phonies. I have seen the transformation of tennis from an elite sport into a big business reaching a very wide and diverse group of people numbering some thirty million players in the United States If I was at all instrumental in helping promote the democratization of tennis, I am proud of this; but I also realize that making tennis accessible to the average person has created the opportunity for exploitation.

Now, as I look back over my seventy-five years of participation in virtually every phase of the game of tennis, as player, teacher, entrepreneur, diplomat, coach, writer, consultant, lecturer, and collector, I see both the good and bad aspects of the changes that have occurred over this long period of time. The danger in the future lies in letting the game, as well as the entire sports structure associated with tennis, spin out of control. This means reining in those who would try to make more out of tennis than the wonderful game it is—be it parents, coaches, agents, manufacturers, promoters, or others who might profit at the expense of younger players. After all, it is only a game.

St. Albans Tennis Club

Membership, 1962

Albright, Mr. and Mrs. Joseph M. P.
Alderton, Mr. Roderick
Baldridge, Miss Letitia
Beyer, Mr. and Mrs. Milton
Borwick, Mr. and Mrs. Richard
Brandon, Mr. Henry O.
Bronz, Mr. and Mrs. George
Browne, Mr. and Mrs. Luis F. V.
Bundy, Mr. and Mrs. McGeorge
Bundy, Mr. and Mrs. William P.
Burch, Mr. Ben D.
Burden, Mrs. W. Douglas
Cary, Mr. and Mrs. William L.
Charbonneaux, Marie Antoinette
Clark, Mr. and Mrs. E. Harrison
Clark, Mr. and Mrs. Joseph S.
Cornell, Mr. and Mrs. Mark

Craig, Mr. Paul M.
Creyke, Mr. and Mrs. Thomas
Cummings, Mr. and Mrs. H. J.
Davids, Mr. Steven Spencer
Day, Dr. Juliana
Dembitz, Mr. and Mrs. Lewis N.
Dinerman, Mr. and Mrs. Samuel
Dreier, Mr. John C.
Eisenstein, Mr. and Mrs. Julian
Fenton, Miss Patricia
Fleming, Mr. Carson
Foster, Mr. and Mrs. Rockwood
Friedman, Mr. and Mrs. Joseph B.
Goldy, Mr. and Mrs. Daniel L.
Gottfried, Mr. and Mrs. Paul M.
Graham, Mrs. Philip L.
Greer, Mr. and Mrs. William H., Jr.
Groberg, Mr. Robert
Harris, Mr. and Mrs. Russell L.
Haselton, Mr. George
Hewes, Mr. and Mrs. Laurence Ilsley
Hodgdon, Mr. and Mrs. A. Dana
Hodgdon, Mrs. Dorothy
Howar, Mr. Edmond
Huyler, Mr. Coulter Dunham, Jr.
Jewett, Mr. and Mrs. Freeborn Garrettson
Kase, Dr. F. J. and Dr. K. A.
Kennedy, Mr. and Mrs. John H.
Kotz, Mr. and Mrs. Arnold

Kuhl, Mr. and Mrs. Nevin E.
Lamont, Mr. and Mrs. Lansing
LeBaron, Mr. and Mrs. Robert
Levine, Miss Selma M.
Lewis, Mr. and Mrs. C. McKenzie, Jr.
Louchheim, Mrs. Katie
Lowrey, Mr. Burling H.
Manning, Mr. and Mrs. Robert J.
Martin, Mr. and Mrs. William McC., Jr.
Marvin, Mr. Langdon
Mathews, Mr. and Mrs. Craig
Mayer, Mr. and Mrs. Charles T.
McNamara, Mr. and Mrs. Robert
McNaughton, Mr. and Mrs. John T.
Meyer, Miss Barbara Lee
Miller, Mr. and Mrs. Leigh M.
Mirza, Humayun
Moorhead, Mr. and Mrs. William S.
Munroe, Mr. and Mrs. Henry
Najar, Mr. Andre
Newhouse, Mr. and Mrs. John
Nurick, Mr. and Mrs. Lester
O'Brien, Miss Anna Belle
Oppenheimer, Mr. and Mrs. Franz M.
Osnos, Mr. and Mrs. Ronald
Panzer, Mr. Irving R. M.
Pell, Mr. and Mrs. Claiborne
Powell, Mr. and Mrs. John W. G.
Prosterman, Mr. and Mrs. Albert M.

Reich, Mr. and Mrs. David
Reid, Miss Hope
Reiter, Mr. Robert H.
Rice, Mrs. Josephine T.
Roosevelt, Mr. and Mrs. Kermit
Rosenberg, Dr. and Mrs. Seymour J.
Rosenfeld, Mr. Samuel J.
Ross, Mr. Thomas B.
Rothwell, Mr. and Mrs. Bruce
Sadove, Mr. Robert
Sagalyn, Mr. and Mrs. Arnold
Schlesinger, Mr. and Mrs. Arthur
Schlosberg, Mrs. Bruce
Scoon, Mr. and Mrs. John G. H.
Seamans, Mr. and Mrs. Robert C., Jr.
Shane, Mr. and Mrs. Presson S.
Shatton, Mr. Alexander
Sitton, Mr. and Mrs. Paul L.
Smoot, Mr. Charles Effinger
Stanley, Mr. and Mrs. Timothy
Sundlun, Mr. and Mrs. Bruce G.
Symington, Mr. and Mrs. James W.
Taft, Mr. and Mrs. William H., III
Taube, Dr. and Mrs. Mortimer
Taylor, Mr. and Mrs. Allen
Temko, Mr. and Mrs. Stanley L.
Thaler, Mr. Martin S.
Thompson, Mr. and Mrs. Tyler
Tiger, Mr. Louis, Jr.

Tirana, Turhan
Topping, Miss Frances K.
Trowbridge, Mr. and Mrs. A. B.
Tyson, Mr. William S.
Vance, Mr. and Mrs. Cyrus R.
Wadden, Mr. Thomas A., Jr.
Wagley, Mr. John
Wallace, Mr. and Mrs. John F.
Wanamaker, Mr. and Mrs. Temple
Warnke, Mr. and Mrs. Paul C.
Weaver, Mrs. M. Parker
Werkman, Dr. Sidney L.
Wilkes, Dr. J. Daniel
Wilson, Mr. Donald M.
Wilson, Mr. and Mrs. Geoffrey M.
Wilson, Mr. Robert
Wise, Mr. David
Woolsey, Mr. and Mrs. Mark H.
Wright, Mr. Hollis C., Jr.
Yungblut, Mr. and Mrs. Charles W.
Zentay, Mr. John

Index